THE YOGIC DHARMA

THE YOGIC DHARMA

The Supreme Yamas and Niyamas

SANTATAGAMANA

Copyright © 2019 by SantataGamana
All rights reserved.
1st Edition, October 2019

ISBN: 978-1699799307

No portion of this book may be reproduced in any form, including photocopying, recording, or any electronic or mechanical methods, without permission from the author except for brief quotes.

Editor: Eric Robins

Design art: Kwaczek/Shutterstock.com, Jozef Klopacka/Shutterstock.com, IvanDbajo/Shutterstock.com

Disclaimer for Legal Purposes

The information provided in this book is strictly for reference only and is not in any manner a substitute for medical advice. In the case of any doubt, please contact your healthcare provider. The author assumes no responsibility or liability for any injuries, negative consequences or losses that may result from practicing what is described in this book. Any perceived slights of specific people or organizations are unintentional. All the names referred to in this book are for illustrative purposes only, are the property of their respective owners and not affiliated with this publication in any way.

Read also, by the same author of *The Yogic Dharma*:

— **KRIYA YOGA EXPOSED**

The Truth About Current Kriya Yoga Gurus & Organizations.

— **THE SECRET POWER OF KRIYA YOGA**

Revealing the Fastest Path to Enlightenment. How Fusing Bhakti & Jnana Yoga into Kriya will Unleash the most Powerful Yoga Ever.

— **KUNDALINI EXPOSED**

Disclosing the Cosmic Mystery of Kundalini. The Ultimate Guide to Kundalini Yoga & Kundalini Awakening.

— **THE YOGA OF CONSCIOUSNESS**

25 Direct Practices to Enlightenment. Revealing the Missing Key to Self-Realization. Beyond Kundalini, Kriya Yoga & all Spirituality into Awakening Non-Duality.

— **TURIYA: THE GOD STATE**

Unravel the ancient mystery of Turiya - The God State. The book that demystifies and uncovers the true state of Enlightened beings.

— **SAMADHI: THE FORGOTTEN EDEN**

Revealing the Ancient Yogic Art of Samadhi.

Available @ Amazon as Kindle & Paperback.

Subscribe and receive the ebook **Uncovering the Real** plus updates and information regarding new books or articles, which will be sent about once a month.

www.RealYoga.info

If you have any doubts or questions regarding this or any of the other books, feel free to contact me at:

Santata@RealYoga.info

Special thanks to Eric Robins, who edited and proofread this book with profound love, kindness, and dedication. Your help has been invaluable.

Whoever finds the meaning of these sayings will not taste death.

- Jesus Christ

TABLE OF CONTENTS

Introduction   **11**

YAMAS

1. Ahimsa — The White Swan   19
   1.1 Kindness Paves the Way   24

2. Satya — The Spiritual Serum   33
   2.1 The Blazing Desire   36

3. Asteya — The Biggest Robbery   43
   3.1 A Cup of Milk   44

4. Brahmacharya — The Unnaturalness of Celibacy   49
   4.1 Brahmawareness   55
   4.2 Abiding in the Unlocalizable   58

5. Aparigraha — Purchasing Delight   63
   5.1 Why do I Want What I Want?   67
   5.2 Your Mind is the Ruler of Value   73

NIYAMAS

6. Sauca — The Whole-Being Detox   79

6.1 The Importance of Taking Good Care of the Body	80
6.2 Interaction With Others in our Spiritual Journey	84
6.3 Inner Cleanse	88
6.4 The Pragmatic Extermination of Beliefs	93
7. Santosa — The Virtuosity of Contentment	99
7.1 Am I in control?	104
7.2 From Drifting to Controlling to Dancing	108
8. Tapas — The Art of Egg Hatching	113
8.1 Spiritual Practice is the Golden Shining Jewel	116
8.2 When Tapas Is All There Is	121
9. Svadhyaya — The University of Being	125
9.1 We Are Not The Children of Dead Matter	126
9.2 Finding Out the "Me" That You Are	133
10. Ishvara Pranidhana — The Relinquishment	141
10.1 God is not a Celebrity	143
10.2 The Science or Art of Self-Realization?	146
10.3 The Truth about Grace	151
11. The Eternal Lion	153
Glossary	**161**

INTRODUCTION

There are various books and information on the internet about what the Yamas and Niyamas are. What they propose is the following:

Yamas = abstentions, moral guidelines, restraints for proper conduct, "don'ts;"

and

Niyamas = ethical observances, positive duties, "dos."

Yet let's be honest: nobody really cares about the Yamas and Niyamas. Reading about them is often tedious, dense, and impractical.

But this book is different. It's not what you think it will be.

While there's no doubt that the teachings found elsewhere may contain useful explanations on the Yamas and Niyamas, they often parrot each other with the typical superficial observances, abstentions, codes of restraint, "dos," and "don'ts." Or they excessively emphasize how practicing celibacy and faithfully reading archaically translated scriptures are the cornerstones of proper Yoga and spiritual practice.

This is not to say that these things don't have their purpose—they do. But we want to go beyond an exposition on ethical or moral concepts. This is especially true considering that learning about the first two limbs of the Yoga Sutras, the Yamas and Niyamas, when they are presented in a distorted, westernized, or over-theorized manner, which is oftentimes embellished to fit today's "self-help chocolate" reading culture, helps very few genuine seekers advance in their spiritual journey of self-transcendence.

Furthermore, it is in Yoga that we often find some of the most highly sectarian organizations and practitioners. I can't fathom how countless members of yoga-based spiritual organizations fight between themselves to gain recognition as the best spiritual organization. But Yoga doesn't need more division, and it must stay faithful to its literal meaning: *union*.

That's one of the things I intended to accomplish with this book: to expose a deeper and unified framework of understanding concerning the Yamas and Niyamas, as these are often mentioned as the foundations of genuine Yoga.

I don't want to entertain more "yogic thought" with this book. Yoga is not about taking ownership of your life and directing it toward the fulfillment that you think you seek. This is because what you truly seek, you will not find in life as you currently know it. No job, no amount of success, no romantic relationship, not a single thing in this world will bring you the fulfillment that you really seek. And in authentic yoga, you don't want to take ownership of your life—you want to surrender it to the Higher Power: God, pure Consciousness, true Self, whatever name you wish to call it. This subject has never been truly taught from this higher perspective.

You won't find many references or extensive thesis-like commentaries in this work either. Its purpose is not to intellectually stimulate you, but to prod you into awakening a deeper desire, an intention, and a power to establish the fertile grounds from which you can realize your true nature. Those attached to scholarly interpretations that never lead to enlightenment may find this appalling. This book is not for them.

Most commentaries on the Niyamas and Yamas are extremely scholarly or theoretical with no practicality at all; others are no more than "self-development" teachings that make no change whatsoever to any seeker's genuine spiritual path—

perhaps they just slightly help to polish the false self, the ego-mind. How can authentic seekers find anything truly precious in these types of teachings?

When the call to write about the Yamas and Niyamas appeared in my consciousness, it came from out of the blue. I never intended to write about them. Truthfully, it is my direct experience (and what I've observed in many seekers) that most of these "codes of proper conduct" naturally arise in a purified, tranquil, and wise mind. Spiritual practice produces a spiritually mature mind, capable of actualizing the Yamas and Niyamas as if they were second nature, which is much better than forcing a seeker to employ these conducts in order to be able to meditate. Paramahansa Yogananda shared this same line of teaching with his disciples. To meditate, we want to relax and let go of noise—we don't need tension and more things filling our minds.

Yet I was compelled to write this book, and after finishing it, I fully understood why. It pushes the understanding of the Yamas and Niyamas further than ever before, expanding their meaning and incorporating a practical aspect onto them rather than merely being a moral and ethical teaching. We'll explore them at their very essence, going beyond all superficial and even conventional understandings.

Prepare yourself for an insightful, pragmatic, and spiritually maturing exposition on Yogic Dharma principles—like you've never seen before. You'll experience a total recontextualization of the Yamas and Niyamas, and rather than applying them as the moral and ethical bedrock of Yoga practice, they will be used as tools for Self-Realization.

Now that's what a real twist is, and hopefully, one that will unleash a powerful roar in your heart.

> "When you run after your thoughts, you are like a dog chasing a stick: every time a stick is thrown, you run after it. Instead, be like a lion who, rather than chasing after the stick, turns to face the thrower. One only throws a stick at a lion once."
>
> - MILAREPA

That thrower is the ego-mind. You are the lion. It is time to set the lion free!

CHAPTER 1

AHIMSA
THE WHITE SWAN

This first Yama is usually thought of as "nonviolence" or "not causing/inflicting pain/harm." *Himsa* means injury or harm, and in Sanskrit, adding an "a" prior to the word turns it into its opposite.

It is usually understood as a call for not directing any kind of violence (physical, emotional, verbal) toward any other living being, at any time. But I don't expect readers of this type of book to be resorting to physical or verbal violence to solve any of their problems. So this obvious type of teaching is not what we're looking for with this book.

Finer comprehensions of this Yama show that "nonviolence" is context-dependent. In other words, a genuine guru yelling at his disciple is not necessarily exhibiting verbal violence—it may actually be a truthful call for awakening; a shaking off that the disciple really required in order to thin out the ego. So in this context, it could be considered as an act of kindness.

An entirely different example is one seen in the therapeutic setting. If a psychologist is helping a patient to overcome mental-emotional distress, she may ask her patient to recall the events that led to his emotional trauma. She may stop him and ask him for intricate, painful details that may cause a great deal of suffering in the moment. She's making her patient relive his trauma! This could be classified as "emotional violence," yet its deeper purpose is to free the patient from that heavy burden. Or alternatively, if a dangerous insect is about to sting your son or daughter, would you kill it or not? There are countless ethical questions regarding what qualifies as violence or nonviolence. It's not as black and white as most pundits make it out to be.

Some traditions espouse extreme constraints regarding this Yama, such as dictating that their ascetic followers must sweep the path ahead of them as they walk in order to prevent them from killing any insect or microscopic creature; or that they wear fine wire mesh masks over their mouths to avert accidentally inhaling some small flying bug. Many of their followers end up totally losing their minds, and some even fast to death as a way of preventing the destruction of other creatures. This is terrible dogmatic trash, and it blocks them from seeing that they are inflicting tremendous amounts of self-violence and, subsequently, not helping anything or anyone in the world at all. They probably aren't even aware that innumerable microorganisms live in their body, and therefore they are inadvertently killing those very same life-forms they've sworn not to kill. It's a total disregard of common sense, which is a plague that often inundates spiritual practitioners in so many myriad ways.

We have to go deeper into the understanding of this Yama so that we can unveil its subtler significance. Beyond not hurting or not "practicing violence" toward others, you mustn't hurt or "practice violence" against yourself[1]. And I'm not talking about physical self-hurt, but about continuing to live a life where you neglect or not fulfill your highest potential, while also ignoring your heart's call for genuine dedication to the eternal Truth.

In countless commentaries on the Yoga Sutras, this Yama is typically given great importance, carrying more weight than the others, being the first on the list and providing the foundation for the rest of the Yamas. You could say that all Yamas are just an expansion of Ahimsa because it lays the groundwork for every other Yama.

---

[1] If your foundations and actions are strongly rooted in truth and love, then you will also be less likely to hurt others in any form.

Ahimsa is about righteousness, or what the Buddha called *Dharma*.

And what is righteousness? It's not about morals, because that too would depend on culture, background, and context. Righteousness is about living life as the purest expression of the Truth that your body-mind vehicle possibly can; living life as if every day were a fresh joy, rather than as if it were a heavy burden limiting your freedom.

If you are reading this book, then you are probably seeking something beyond; something to free you from all forms of suffering; something that will grant you eternal bliss; something that will allow you to rest in peace while still alive; something that will grant you profound insights and wisdom. Perhaps it's about complete love or perfect fulfillment, or about understanding your place in the world and what you truly are, or what life, the universe, and God are all about. Or maybe you just don't want any more misery and suffering —you've had enough. These are all noble pursuits, the most auspicious ones that one could have in a lifetime.

Every time you are performing an action (including speech or thought) that goes *toward* the direction of realizing the aforementioned, then you are on the path of light; every time you perform an action that goes *backward* in the direction of realizing the aforementioned, you are inflicting violence against yourself and the world.

Ignoring your true Self (pure consciousness) is the subtlest form of violence, harm, and egotism. Ignoring your true Self is neglecting the Yama of Ahimsa.

The practice of yogic non-violence (Ahimsa) is nothing more than having a tranquil mind free from inauspicious thoughts, and our whole being emanating kindness and love.

Thus, there's no better way to begin the practice of Ahimsa than by cultivating the opposite of *himsa* (violence): kindness.

KINDNESS PAVES THE WAY

Do not let this be just another day where you selfishly go through life. Make this day different. Perform a gesture of kindness, smile at someone, or do something along these lines.

You may initially meet some mental resistance, and your mind may see this as something that requires tremendous effort, but that's just nonsense. Don't listen to the mind. Do an act of kindness. You will feel good about it. Don't let all this just be theory and concepts—make it practical.

It doesn't matter what it is. It may even be that *thing* that you've wanted to do for so long for someone that you know, but that you have subconsciously postponed indefinitely.

Lots of people feel that nothing good happens to them. This propels them to live in a self-fulfilling cycle of defeatist thinking, sentimental anguish, and a dreary attitude toward life. The truth is that a simple act of kindness from a random stranger may change just that. This is such a simple step, yet is one that can set in motion something much bigger than that singular act of kindness.

Oftentimes, our act of kindness will produce a "domino effect," generating a chain reaction of kindness across the globe, because the recipient of the altruistic act will be consciously or unconsciously inspired to perpetuate it for others. If you perform a genuine act of kindness toward a person, and they truly feel gratitude, in that very moment the barriers of the separate self of that person will temporarily become more translucent—you are giving them a glimpse of freedom and joy.

Kindness is how we would naturally act if we didn't feel like we were a separate being[2]. Kindness is one of the melodies of Oneness. It's a way of reconnecting with your "larger Self." Just like in a dream everything and everyone is part of you—a manifestation of you (the dreamer, your mind)—in this world it's all part of you as well, but as consciousness. How can you be anything but compassionate and kind?

Kindness is giving light to those who may think they are alone. Kindness is the most powerful way to practice Ahimsa. It counters *himsa*.

Perform an act of kindness. And don't expect anything in return. You're just going to be full-heartedly kind. Do it.

---

[2] But remember what was written earlier about kindness not being as black and white as it may initially seem. Kindness is the act of being kind; a hurt dog may try to bite you if you try to treat/help it. You are being kind, but the dog doesn't know it. The attitude and behavior of a genuine guru will always be in the direction of the Truth, even if the student may perceive it as something "painful."

"Kindness is the language which the deaf can hear and the blind can see."

- MARK TWAIN

* * *

Have you done an act of kindness? How did it feel? (If you didn't manage to do it yet, go back and try again. You can keep reading, but please, do it before going onto the next chapter.)

Notice how you feel about the act of kindness that you did. Does it feel good?

Dwell for a bit on those sensations. Get to know their "feeling tone."

As we progress on the spiritual path, the desire to become more loving and compassionate arises within.

There is much conflict in the world, and the most varied "frequencies." We want to begin to attune to and then bathe ourselves in the frequency of love. This is important for our spiritual path.

This love that I'm mentioning is not a personal love. It is not love for anything or for anyone in particular, but rather love as a state of being. Love and kindness are natural by-products of an egoless consciousness, and the more we dissipate and let go of our ego, the more effortless it is to be kind and loving. When you are in a state of love, you are more recipient to be kind; when you are in a state of kindness, you are more recipient to love. In either state, the ego is diminished.

Practicing love and kindness toward ourselves by bathing in this energy is extremely important, because they have the ability to eradicate separation from our lives.

The "feeling" of love and kindness that you felt can be translated into a "connection." Love-kindness is the feeling of connection to one another. The more we realize our interconnectedness, the more we vibrate in the frequency of love and kindness. The more we vibrate in the frequency of love and kindness, the more we realize our interconnectedness. The more we realize our interconnectedness, the more we realize how thin our finite self's barriers are. That's why you should practice Self-love and Self-kindness.

It is so easy to tell a lie, to hurt one another, or to be dismissive of others. Self-love and Self-kindness are not what you'd usually consider them to be. To practice them, we must actually love Self and be kind to Self, and this is not referring to the ego-self. How do we accomplish this?

"Self" is not an entity, but rather it's our true Being. So when we stay just being, loving just being, we are being kind to ourselves—we are giving us (as awareness) the attention we require and deserve. Rarely have human beings paid attention to, let alone loved, their own awareness.

So, here's what you should do:

At least for the duration of this book, you will take 5 minutes every day, either right after waking up, or right before falling asleep, to focus on this feeling and experience of kindness. If the previous attempt didn't go as planned, it's okay. Try to do it again, or try to remember the last time you performed some spontaneous act of kindness and use that feeling tone.

Invite a sense of kindness, love, acceptance, joy, and gratitude into your heart. Then, let the feeling of kindness and love radiate from your heart, filling your whole being. Evoke warm-heartedness and let your heart melt into kindness and compassion. Bathe yourself in this energy, drink from this eternal fountain, taste this divine nectar, regenerate, and invigorate yourself in this temple of God. It is a healing practice.

As you keep practicing it, you will get better at recreating the inner experience of kindness, which will help kick-start your day with a feeling of kindness, gratitude, and love. It just takes 5 minutes, and the cumulative effect will be real if properly done.

What better way to start your day?

Alternatively, you can do this right before you perform your meditation or spiritual practice. You can recall the pleasant feeling of kindness for 5 minutes, expanding it from your heart toward the rest of the body. This will improve your spiritual practice ten-fold.[3]

As a consequence of this kindness practice, a sincere beauty will radiate forth from your whole body-mind system. Your face will appear less heavy, more spacious, more peaceful, and emit a shining glow. It will emanate joy, kindness, and authenticity.

When someone is full of anger or meanness, the way they stand, move, talk, act, eat, etc., is clearly shown. It quickly ages their bodies. The relentless flood of cortisol and other stress chemicals in the body of such a person lead to higher blood pressure and metabolic rate, increased inflammation,

---

[3] This alternate instruction is not entirely different from applying *bhakti* (devotion) into your sadhana. It uses the same principle of breaking the "mechanical-ness" of the practice by starting first with a foundation of love and devotional energy, which improves the ability to concentrate and the pleasantness experienced, conditioning the mind to engross itself even further into the practice.

impaired immune function, more wrinkles and frown lines, and may even upset regular sensory, neural and hormonal mechanisms. Being unkind and unloving toward oneself, and consequently toward others, often leads to a host of health issues. This is *himsa*, harm, or violence.

Being loving and kind brings our mind to a serene state of being because it generates calmness and spaciousness. When we step out of our ego-mind agenda, we become freer and more gracious. Life seems to become more united; kindness and love slowly become our bedrock. Actions begin to come from within, in symphony with our spiritual path and positively impacting not only our life but also the lives of those around us.

When pure love and kindness are experienced, everything else is thrown away. While immersed in divine love, you won't think about liberation, enlightenment, practicing, *samadhi*, etc. All of these are thrown out of the window. Why would you care for anything if you are pure love? That's pure bliss!

Once you experience kindness and love at their core, you'll realize that they are pure bliss. After such an experience, this bliss leaves a powerful trace in your heart, emanating its fragrance everywhere. That's how you are supposed to start your day—with the perfume of the Divine.

"My religion is kindness."

- THE 14TH DALAI LAMA

CHAPTER 2

SATYA
THE SPIRITUAL SERUM

Satya means Truth. In yogic terms, as a Yama, it is commonly known as Truthfulness, and it implies that the practitioner must take a vow to do one's best not to lie in terms of actions, speech, and thought.

One could apply this principle by following these three methods:

1. Being tremendously lucid and aware of one's words before speaking. Whenever you are about to speak, pause for a few seconds, and internally ask yourself before speaking: "Is what I'm going to say coming from authenticity, genuineness?" If so, speak ahead. If not, do not speak.

2. Being extremely attentive to one's actions before performing them. In other words, rather than acting on auto-pilot, be aware of what you are doing and its implications.

3. Remaining within the "field of truthfulness," which will make your thoughts attune to a more truthful frequency, thereby self-purifying.

Basically, it's about not being inauthentic, not even in the small things. In the end, it's not just about not *telling* lies, but about not *being* a lie. This, in itself, is a powerful teaching to attempt to adopt, even if only for a day, but preferably, as a lasting principle.

In fact, there is no need to lie about anything because you are not trying to defend an illusion or anything at all. Furthermore, there's an inherent beauty to being truthful, to which people and even the universe respond to favorably. Being grounded in truthfulness is a stepping-stone toward the realization of the ultimate Truth.

With that being said, there's even more depth to this Yama of Truthfulness. It's about the desire for Freedom and keeping yourself truthful to the choice you made to attain it.

Whenever I hear or read about someone saying that all they want is to find their real nature, find what or who God is, or to be enlightened and bathed in eternal bliss, the vast majority of the time, such is not true. Those words do not come from a place of realness and truthfulness, but rather from the ego.

Their desire to find out the Truth is not real enough; they

still haven't truly made the choice. And this burning desire is one of the most critical aspects of success on the spiritual path. If it's not burning and real, then you are not following the principle of Satya. You are merely lying to yourself.

It is written that Jesus said, "The Truth will set you free." When we're talking about the supreme Truth, this is completely true. However, I've found that there is a caveat on this axiom: the Truth will set you free, but only if you genuinely want it!

THE BLAZING DESIRE

All human beings have desires. Desire is a craving for something that appears to be missing in our current experience. It is the conscious or unconscious feeling that something is lacking, and thus, there arises the urge to "move" toward that which will fill up this negative feeling of being "empty" or "lacking." It is thus a lack of recognition of the completeness of the present moment, and an anxiety for the future. It is a rejection of "now" with the hope of embracing "then."

Every time we perform an action, that action produces a memory. Memories have the potential to generate desire, which in turn generates a repeated action (we tend to repeat pleasurable actions as well as actions that enable us to avoid pain and suffering). As long as we keep running in the rat race of desires, we will live a predictable life of mediocrity, always jumping from one desire to another.

When we desire something, we are not fully aware, fully present, fully now. If there were no desires, then nothing would be missing, and maximum joy and peace would be the current state. Desirelessness equals completeness.

Since desiring is an impulse to take action to achieve something, then the desire to be free from all suffering, to enjoy immeasurable ecstasy, to be eternally in peace, or to have access to unfathomable realms of profound wisdom, is also an impulse to take action to move from what is currently lacking toward what we desire.

However, there is a difference between the desire to be Self-Realized or enlightened in comparison to all others: we are desiring to achieve *That* which ends all desires once and for all.

The explanation of how a desire can end all desires can be found in Kundalini Exposed chapter 5 "The Alchemy of the Instinct":

> That super intense desire [for Self-Realization] is unlike all other desires because it will burn them all, like a burning log that will consume all the other logs when placed together. That burning desire is the main factor that will determine whether or not you will become liberated. Yes, the intensity of your desire is that important—without it, you will not go far. It is what distinguishes real aspirants from wannabe seekers.

To distinguish this desire from all other desires, we'll refer to it as the "urge for enlightenment."

This urge is fundamental. It is the number one requisite for enlightenment, yet is one of the most neglected dictums. If this desire to be free does not saturate and encompass your whole being every single day, then you are not employing the principle of Satya. You are being untruthful to yourself.

Many seekers start out with lots of motivation and with a genuine intention to attain Freedom. With time, however, this intensity and desire begin to fade into oblivion. Don't allow this to happen. As the desire for Freedom dissipates into the background, superficial desires involving more immediate gratification begin to arise in the foreground. If you say that you want to be enlightened and realize your true nature, but then your actions, speech, and thoughts do not reflect that, then you are merely deceiving yourself—you are being untruthful to your heart's deepest desire.

The best way to overcome this is to cultivate the urge for enlightenment. One of the ways to do it is through discernment or discrimination. The reason that almost all human beings lack both the understanding and the urge for enlightenment is due to a lack of discernment. People think that the value of anything is ingrained or intrinsic to the thing itself. But this is not the case, for if it were, everyone would equally value the same objects, events, persons, circumstances, etc. And it is not hard to see that we don't. Uncontacted Amazonian tribes couldn't care less about a $20,000 18kt gold ring, yet they may find a mirror quite interesting and valuable. A mother of five in Mozambique doesn't attribute any value to Super Bowl VIP tickets, but she would definitely value food and medicine.

It is then easy to see that value is not inherent in anything, except to the person attributing it. We are the value-providers, not the value-finders. We live in a society that collectively values the same things, so we tend to desire those very same things: professional success, social status, physical health and fitness, material wealth, and pleasure-indulging activities.

Due to our lack of recognition that we are the ones who give value to anything, we continuously seek to fill our feeling of lack with the value that achieving all those things will supposedly provide. We overlook enlightenment because we cannot see value in it. But enlightenment is the most valuable achievement in the whole Universe! It is a discovery of our own infinite value.

Furthermore, it is also important to realize that spirituality doesn't mean lack of abundance in all facets of life. It doesn't mean material poverty, having an unfit body, being a professional failure, or that you can't eat pizza, crack a joke, or watch a movie in the cinema. On the contrary, it allows us to actually feel freer to appreciate things in life without inhibition and to fully express ourselves to the best of our ability in whatever it is that we're supposed to do in this world.

Even though enlightenment dramatically changes your worldview, it doesn't diminish enjoyment in the world—it is definitely much more enjoyable, blissful, and totally free of misery.

As you begin to seek enlightenment, a jungle of spiritual concepts, New Age doctrines, and mumbo-jumbo practices will appear. Instead of losing yourself in all of that, always remember to stick to the essentials:

1- Read dogma-free spiritual books that inspire and motivate you to increase your urge for enlightenment;

2- Engage in genuine spiritual practice to discover the light within that illuminates the darkness of illusion;

3- Connect and be physically, mentally, or spiritually in the presence of an awakened one;

The more you do this, the more your life will be attuned to the Yama of Satya. And the more attuned your life is to the Yama of Satya, the more God leads you to the realization of your own true Self.

Above all, the urge for enlightenment is incredibly critical.

If you say that you want to be the best piano player in the world, yet you rarely play the piano, is that desire really true? If you say that you want to run a marathon, yet you rarely train, is that desire really true? If you say you've always had a dream of visiting Stonehenge, yet you keep splurging money on useless things instead of buying tickets for your travel, is that dream or desire really true?

The same principle applies here. Just because someone says they want to achieve Freedom, that doesn't mean it's true. What they want is to achieve what they believe Freedom is. And when it doesn't happen in the timeframe they think it should, they become unmotivated and give up. But spirituality is not a magic-pill game—it's the most profound endeavor of the human kingdom.

Though I'm comparing the desire for enlightenment to other desires, they are nothing alike. Other desires will always leave you wanting more because they will never bring the eternal fulfillment that you ultimately seek.

This urge to be free of lies and ignorance and to constantly bathe in the sun of Consciousness, on the other hand, will transform your burning log of intense desire for enlightenment into a gigantic flame that will consume all of the other logs (desires).

It is time to discover the root of all your desires—the desire to be complete, happy, and at peace. May all of your desires merge into this one desire, and then with single-pointed determination, the most auspicious conquest of the human kingdom will, at last, be achieved.

If you are genuine about your spiritual path, your whole life must be an expression of this. That is abiding by Satya, one of the foundations of Yoga. It's staying true to your highest potential; true to your heart's deepest call; true to yourself.

That's your mission.

CHAPTER 3

ASTEYA
THE BIGGEST ROBBERY

Asteya, which is composed of "a" (non-) plus *steya* (act of stealing), translates into "non-stealing." This is not about stealing money or robbing from others—you don't need a book to tell you that you definitely shouldn't do that. This is about not stealing your highest potential from yourself.

If there's one thing we all don't get back, it is time. Whether we like it or not, time passes on. Time is the ultimate destroyer of all things in this relative universe. Nothing in this dual existence can overcome time. Time is *Yama*[4], *the* Hindu god of death.

So why do you keep stealing your own inner treasure from yourself by postponing happiness and freedom (your ultimate goals)? Why do you keep acting like there's enough time?

---

[4] Not to be confused with the Yamas that we're exploring here.

There's a story about a man that stole himself of his own realization.

A Cup of Milk

There was a young man who seemed to be quite sincere, and for many years all he wanted was to become enlightened. He had read some sacred scriptures and had a basic understanding of what enlightenment and the spiritual path entail. This knowledge, alongside an urge to be free of Maya, can be quite powerful. But he wanted a guru because he felt he couldn't do it all by himself and wanted some help and direction. So he went around searching for one until he heard a tale of an enlightened guru living in the jungle.

He promptly packed his stuff and went to that said jungle to find the enlightened guru.

After wandering for a few days, he finally found someone in the heart of the jungle, just quietly sitting. This had to be the enlightened guru he had heard about—he could feel it. The guru's aura was bright and strong.

As he approached the enlightened guru, the young man humbly prostrated and asked him to teach him the path toward enlightenment.

"You still aren't ready. Maya will trick you into ignorance," said the guru.

"I am ready Master. Please teach me," supplicated the man.

The guru looked at him and nodded his head.

"Ok, I'll teach you—but first, please, go get me a cup of milk. I haven't eaten or drunk anything in many days."

So the young man set out across the jungle to the nearest village to get a cup of milk. The sun was blazing hot at that time of the day, and he couldn't seem to find a way out of the jungle. The heat was becoming too much, the man was tired, and his stomach also began to wish for a cup of milk.

Suddenly, he saw a dog running around in this remote place; he found this weird, and so he started following the dog. He noticed that the dog had a collar, and this piqued his curiosity even more.

After spending around 10 minutes chasing the dog, he noticed that he was nearing the edge of the jungle, close to a village. He looked ahead and saw a beautiful young woman who was the dog's owner. As soon as she smiled at him, he was captivated by her beauty and fell in love.

Eventually, they wound up getting married. Since she came from a wealthy family, the man ended up working for the family business. Children soon arrived, and then grandchildren. The man eventually became a great patriarch of his large family, admired by the entire village.

Decades went by, until one year his wife got sick and ended up passing away. Unfortunately, the man from our story couldn't overcome his grief and fell into a prolonged depression.

One day, as he was walking by the village, he gazed over and saw a man milking a cow. This jogged his memory and he suddenly recalled the cup of milk his guru had asked him to fetch decades before.

He began running as best as his old body would allow in the direction of the jungle. It wasn't easy, he was sweating, and his breathing was difficult as he gasped for oxygen. He went straight through the jungle, directly to the spot that his faint memory recollected from decades prior.

After a few minutes, he suddenly saw the figure of the guru. He didn't seem to have aged at all.

"So, have you brought me a cup of milk? I'm starving. What took you so long?"

"Maya, dear Master. I'm so sorry. I see now the intricate web that I was entangled in."

His weak heart was pounding from the run and from the

shock of finding his guru still waiting there for him. Suddenly, as he was looking at the Master and feeling utter disappointment in himself for his own forgetfulness, he saw the Master's facial features reflect the face of *Yama*, the Hindu god of death. The man's time had come and he knew it. He took one last deep breath, closed his eyes, and his body died on the spot.

He had stolen himself of his own spiritual progress in this lifetime due to his forgetfulness. It's not that one can't live life and still be enlightened—it's about not letting the web of Maya envelop you in this dream, stealing you of your inner treasure. If you're not looking at the light, you're looking at *Yama*.

After all, forgetfulness of our spiritual nature and path can only lead to the darkness of ignorance—the prison of time—which always results in death. Don't let anything in the web of Maya trap you and rob you of your own inner wealth. Don't be like the man in this story.

The pleasures in this world are always temporary. Your true Self is eternal life. And guess what, if our protagonist had brought that beautiful young woman back to the guru along with the cup of milk, perhaps they could have both overcome Maya together. He ended up stealing both his and his wife's chances at Self-Realization.

If he had taken a step back for a moment, just long enough to reflect on his inner dimension, he might've remembered sooner about his guru in the jungle. This introspection would have taken him from unconsciousness and forgetfulness to consciousness and lucidity. That could have altered the course of his life. Self-introspection is critical, otherwise one can go years or even lifetimes without advancing a single step on their spiritual path.

The purpose of this lesson is to help remind you of what is truly important. Live your life, take care of your responsibilities, do what you have to do, but at no point must you ever forget to always move in the direction of fulfilling your highest potential—realizing your true eternal nature.

Ultimately, this is the most significant decision in your life, one that you will have to consciously reaffirm every day in order to prevent Maya from taking over and stealing you of your divine bliss.

CHAPTER 4

Brahmacharya
The Unnaturalness of Celibacy

Brahmacharya is probably the most misunderstood principle of the whole Yamas & Niyamas.

In typical yogic literature, it is a call for celibacy. They say that by preserving your sexual energy, you can build up a powerful reservoir to use in spiritual practice. Despite this interpretation not being the real meaning of Brahmacharya, the basic principles it espouses are true, though they come with many caveats.

First of all, conserving your sexual energy can turn into repression of libido, which is essentially an oppression of your own human and sexual nature. This is terrible, and can have tremendous adverse effects both on the body and on the psyche. It's a billion times better to act naturally rather than to repress your sexual energy.

> "The more prohibitions you have, the less virtuous people will be."
>
> - Lao Tzu,
> Tao Te Ching (Stephen Mitchell translation)

Unless you are practicing a form of energetic alchemy, which transforms sexual desire into spiritual desire by elevating the life-force from the lower energy centers (root and sacral chakras) into the higher energy centers (third-eye and crown chakras), then the conservation of sexual energy (Brahmacharya—as it's usually understood) is not for you. It will not be natural. There's no escaping this.

Yoga accomplishes this energetic alchemy through the practice of life-force control (pranayama, or similar techniques). Kriya Yoga achieves this through many of its techniques such as Kriya Pranayama and Maha Mudra; Kundalini Yoga accomplishes this through Kriya Supreme Fire; Tibetan Buddhism through Tummo breathing/Inner Fire awakening; Taoism through different forms of microcosmic or macrocosmic orbit and qi (prana) control/cultivation, etc.

Even if you are practicing these techniques, the amount of sexual energy that is successfully transmuted into a burning desire for enlightenment and spiritual purposes may be relatively low. It depends on your spiritual maturity, lifestyle, and proficiency in applying the techniques.

To simplify this understanding, let's suppose that 10% of your libido is transmuted into spiritual energy. What about the other 90%? If it remains, then this means that there will still be a strong desire for sex (i.e., there is still a lot of sexual energy in your system). Thus you need to be mindful of your bodily needs and functions and act accordingly. There must be no repressing whatsoever. This doesn't mean seekers should release their sexual tension twice a day, or that they should practice strict celibacy. Always aim for the naturalness of the body. Learn to listen to your body.

Typically, if you are consistent in doing your spiritual practice, libido and sexual energy will reduce over time (not necessarily reaching "zero" though), while spiritual hunger, desire, and energy will increase proportionally. That being said, it may also happen that you successfully transmute a "percentage" of your sexual energy into spiritual energy, but due to the nature of energy and kundalini practices, your sexual energy still increases.

In other words, when successfully transmuting sexual energy into spiritual energy, new sexual energy may be generated through the process as a side effect.

This could fuel even more transformation into spiritual energy, but it could also simply increase your base-level of libido. Since sexual energy is just a grosser form of spiritual energy, the art of energetic alchemy is the refining of this sexual energy into its subtler essence—spiritual energy. The reason that new sexual energy may be generated as a by-product is due to the refining process tapping into typically untouched and dormant reservoirs of energy in the lower chakras.

This explains why some seekers may believe that they're not successfully transmuting sexual energy into spiritual energy: because their libido increased or stayed the same. But now you know that this may not be the case.

This is why it may be unwise to have "sleepovers" with ungrounded, immature practitioners in Kundalini-type retreats—you never know what such excess of sexual energy may do to their still "infantile" consciousness.

I cannot overstress this enough: listen to your body and act naturally. Of course, you need to have some self-discipline and attentiveness, but don't turn the teaching of preservation of sexual energy into a hideous suppression.

I can't tell you how many times readers have reached out to me and confided that they were having a hard time controlling their libido. Well, if you oppress and judge it puritanically, you're not doing yourself any good.

The practice of transmutation of sexual energy is important and beginners should 100% abide by it through consistently following their main sadhanas of Kriya Yoga, Kundalini Yoga, etc. Having said so, that's not what the real Yama of Brahmacharya is about. The real meaning of Brahmacharya is abiding in pure Consciousness.

Brahman is a Sanskrit name for God, pure Consciousness or true Self. *Charya* means conduct, engaging, or following. Brahmacharya is living as God, being aware of God at all times. This is a much deeper understanding of this Yama, which requires a great deal of spiritual maturity to employ[5].

Here is Sri Ramana Maharshi's response on this subject:

> "Devotee Question: Isn't brahmacharya necessary?
>
> Ramana Maharshi answer: Brahmacharya means 'living in Brahman'. It has no connection with celibacy as is commonly understood. A real brahmachari finds bliss in Brahman, the same as Self.

---

[5] *Acharya*, on the other hand, means "one who is followed," "one who performs dharma," or more commonly "instructor," "preceptor," or spiritual teacher. Brahman + Acharya would mean Brahman (God) is the one to be followed, the one and only instructor, preceptor, and spiritual teacher.

Devotee: Is naishthika brahmacharya (life-long celibacy) essential as a sadhana for Self-Realisation?

Bhagavan: Realisation itself is naishthika brahmacharya. The vow is not brahmacharya. Life in Brahman is brahmacharya and it is not a forcible attempt at it. To live and move in Brahman is real brahmacharya; continence, of course, is very helpful and indispensable to achieve that end. But so long as you identify yourself with the body, you could never escape sex-thought and distraction. It is only when you realise that you are formless Pure Awareness that sex-distinction disappears for good and that is brahmacharya, effortless and spontaneous."

- Talks with Ramana Maharshi

Let's dig deeper.

Brahmawareness

Let's understand how to employ the Yama of Brahmancharya to its maximum potential.

We all live our lives as if we were going to live forever. But life goes by in the blink of an eye, and we, as the "I-ego," as the personality we believe ourselves to be, will have an end. It doesn't last forever. We may try our best to delay the inevitable, but inevitable means exactly that: unavoidable, inescapable, certain, or sure to happen.

Death is inevitable—we'll all have to face it. There's no possibility of escape. So, right in this very lifetime, we have to discover the timelessness; we have to uncover what is before life, during life, and after life.

Sit down and ponder on one of your earliest memories. Try your best to do this for a few minutes. What does that memory bring up for you? What do you feel? What is it exactly?

I want you to take 10 to 20 minutes to sit or lie down and become aware of that old childhood memory (it may be pleasant or unpleasant, but this type of interpretation is irrelevant to the exercise), preferably of when you were between 4 to 10 years old.

Notice whether you feel that you are the same being or not.

Are you the same now as you were in those events that you are remembering right now? You are most definitely different. There may be no similarities at all. Perhaps you neither like nor dislike the same things now that you used to like and dislike back then; you probably don't have any similar habits; your thinking mind and intellect are totally dissimilar to what they were; your personality has totally changed; your understanding and view of the world are like night and day; and above all, your sense of identity and cognition back then feels very distinct.

But let's take a step back and ponder:

Is awareness feeling different, or are you identifying it with its contents and calling it different?

Can you notice that regardless of how it feels, that which is aware remains the same? The personality (alongside all of its facets) and body which you used to refer to as "I" have changed, but the awareness that is aware of both didn't change.

The sense of being aware is the same. It ever was, is and will be the same. The awareness with which you remember these old events now is the same with which you were experiencing them back then. Only the contents of awareness change, not the awareness itself. "Being aware" doesn't change.

With this in mind, for the next couple of days, I want you to recognize that despite its contents, despite what's going on in your life, despite what happened back then in your memories, despite how you currently feel, your sense of "being aware" is always the same. It is timeless. Discover this timelessness!

It's a recognition of the background of consciousness and an abidance and surrendering "into" it.

Abiding as consciousness itself (i.e., being aware of being aware) is the true meaning of Brahmacharya.

> "All this is Brahman. Everything comes from Brahman, everything goes back to Brahman, and everything is sustained by Brahman. One should therefore quietly meditate on Brahman."[6]
>
> - CHANDOGYA UPANISHAD

---

[6] Substitute the word Brahman here for Consciousness and you have the key to spirituality.

Abiding in the Unlocalizable

Whenever you look for consciousness or for the "I Am" presence, there is always the danger of objectifying it. Because of your long-held habit of constantly identifying "I" with an object, when you go to look for it, you may feel that the "I" is located somewhere in your body, or that it may have some sort of quality or tactile or kinesthetic sensation.

If you do find the "I" somewhere (e.g., you feel it in the head or in the heart), that doesn't mean the "I" is actually there. The "I," which is equated with consciousness or awareness, is that which is aware of what you are aware of. If you find the "I" located somewhere in your body or psyche, then that's not the "I," but rather an ego-knot which awareness ("I") is aware of.

This is precisely the same as if it felt like you found some sensory quality to the "I" (e.g., you feel that it is fuzzy, cloudy, solid, dense, or translucent). In fact, that's not the "I," but rather an ego-knot which awareness ("I") is aware of.

And what is an "ego-knot?" It's that which may accompany the sensation of "I" or of "being" when we try to practice "finding" and "abiding" in it, but it's the "false" part of "I."

By this, I mean the following:

The "I" that we typically believe we are is a mixture of awareness, thoughts, sensations, feelings, and perceptions. It is a mixture of "awareness" and "that which awareness is aware of" (though they're not two different things, I am simplifying to convey a point).

If I believe I am a singular entity, a person, and whose personality could be described as "moody," "shy," and "smart," then whenever I think of "I," I will experience/feel a conglomerate of consciousness (*chit*, sentience, that which is aware) plus that which is insentient (*jada*, that which is an object of awareness), which includes my identity (composed of countless attributes such as "moody," "shy," and "smart," and so on). This "cocktail" can be called "I-ego," ego-mind, or just ego, depending on the context.

If you abide as "I" by just being, then you, as consciousness, are focusing on consciousness. This is the correct nondual practice of *Atma-Vichara* (Self-Inquiry). But if you, as consciousness, focus on the insentient part (the apparent attributes of "I"), then you may end up dissolving those psychological facets in your mind (which is a great purifying practice), but it is not proper nondual practice. It leads to emotional and psychological improvement and evolution, but it doesn't necessarily help to transcend the false self, the "I-ego."

Whenever there is a persistent emotional, psychological, traumatic or subjective issue, there's a corresponding "energetic knot" within our energy/pranic system. Spiritual practice can dissolve such knots and oftentimes, merely by just focusing on them, our power of detached witnessing and mindfulness can dissolve them into infinite expanse. Vipassana-style meditations, where one observes bodily and mental processes, frequently involve this type of psychological release as well. Moreover, doing proper yoga *asanas* or simply consciously tensing and releasing certain body parts can also bring psychological relief by releasing tension in the muscles, because there's often a counterpart in the physical body to the energetic knots (i.e. a "physical knot").

All of this can result in an astonishing psychological purification, but it must not be confused with the "I" or "I am" presence that I refer to. You can integrate both types of practices, but don't replace the latter for the former.

When I say to look for consciousness or awareness or to look for a sense of beingness or "I am" presence, I'm referring to the unlocalizable and unqualified experiencer of all experiences—that which is "aware of," but is in itself, nothing at all.

When you find this unfindable "I," which, paradoxically, is only possible by *being it*, there may be accompanying sensations, perceptions, or feelings that fill this empty awareness. These sensations may be related to mental phenomena, psychological issues, or really anything at all. It's okay if this happens, but just continue to "focus" on the "non-objectifiable" part of "I," which is empty awareness.

For example, if you look for "I" or consciousness and abide in the spaciousness of being, but feel a small perception or sensation in the middle or back of the head, in the heart, or anywhere at all, as if it were a translucent, fuzzy or even dense "speck," this is perfectly fine. Such sensations may accompany this practice until the very end when everything totally drops away. But they are not what the "I" truly points toward—awareness. That's where you have to be!

CHAPTER 5

APARIGRAHA
PURCHASING DELIGHT

The last Yama means "non-greed," "non-grasping," or "non-possessiveness." As you already know, in Sanskrit, adding an "a" prior to the word turns it into its opposite. "Parigraha" means "to crave" or "to seize."

This principle is about not seeking or craving material possessions—an abstention from greed. That's what it's about: non-acquisitiveness.

Now the thing is, everybody has heard or read that a genuine seeker of spirituality should shun all types of possessions and materialism. Theoretically, this is true. But in practice, we come yet again to the issue of oppressing desires. Do you know what happens when you suppress a powerful desire? It consumes you, and it's just a matter of time until it explodes and takes possession of your life. Suppression is never the way forward.

To truly put this Yama into practice, what's required is discernment. This means not forcing desires away, but understanding that what you genuinely desire is not actually what you think it is. If you want a new expensive thing, but your guru forces you to not buy it by saying "You should neither desire nor cling to material objects" (which is true), and you end up not buying it through sheer will, that doesn't mean you've dissipated that desire—it just means that it was pushed back into the subconscious. This untranscended desire will germinate and spread negative seeds through your psyche, and then at some future point, either in meditation or in life, it will come to the forefront and have to be dealt with. Suppression of desires can turn them into powerful monsters.

Most of the time, meditation in and of itself is not enough to awaken the required discernment. You also require strong additional pointers that direct your intellect toward such insight and discernment. These pointers on their own are not enough either, despite what Neo-Advaita contemporary teachers may suggest. Meditation and direct pointers both work together synergistically.

The following chapters will help you to awaken the required insight—they will propel your heart to silently say: "I know this is true." Consciously, you will have no doubts whatsoever. Then, with the help of continued spiritual practice and by reflecting on these pointers, your subconscious will be flooded with this higher level of awareness, leading you to live a life true to what your beingness already knows. That being said, this very rarely occurs in an instant; it's more of a progressive nature, a realization that you slowly grow into and integrate.

However, if there's still a strong remaining desire toward materialism, it's okay. Live your life and fully experience it through the senses. Build a business or get a fantastic job, earn lots of money, buy whatever you wish to buy, get your dream partner, go on vacation to the most exotic and marvelous places, etc. Do everything that you believe will fulfill you. Then, if despite all of this hard work and perseverance you don't succeed in acquiring what you wished for, or once you directly realize that "having it all" will never be enough to bring total fulfillment and permanently cease suffering, you can finally turn to spiritual life and practice.

You can easily realize for yourself how delusional the "love for things" is and how they can trap you into a vicious cycle:

Whenever you obtain some new thing that you adore, observe how you feel after its "honeymoon" period has passed. The initial rush and pleasure you got from that thing begins to fade out until it just becomes another ordinary object. It has lost its value or appeal, and now your mind may desire something different, something better or new. When you get a new iPhone, you treat it with so much care, just like a newborn. A couple of months afterward, you're already throwing it around to the couch or bed.

Did this new thing bring any lasting satisfaction, or did it just provide a temporary anesthesia? It's a fake happiness, one that you will keep pursuing and never finding. Possessions can be like taking cocaine in order to experience a short burst of happiness—but this is fleeting and you'll eventually feel the negative aftereffects. Unfortunately, just like most drugs, the joy experienced when getting new things reinforces the reward pathways in the brain, becoming addictive and creating a sort of dependence. You then want new things in order to continue feeling that pleasure. It's a never-ending cycle; a mirage that you can never reach.

Now, I'm not saying you can't buy or own anything. You obviously can buy whatever you wish. You don't need to be poor or buy cheap things of inferior quality that will not serve you as well. It's just that you must awaken out of this materialistic-trap of *living just to acquire pleasure-giving things you don't really need!*

Why do I Want What I Want?

Why do people want material wealth? Why do people want what they want?

It is because they believe that those things that they want will make them feel complete and happy. Whatever people wish for is just because they believe it will make them happy. What they are really looking for is happiness!

Whenever you desire something new, ask yourself: Why do I want this?

I want you to dig deep into your mind with this question. Why do you want what you want? Why is this desiring emerging in the first place? What void is it going to fill?

Let's suppose Maria longs to find a partner. She's had some relationships before, but they never quite worked out. Now she really wants to find her "soul mate." There's nothing wrong with that, but if she were to investigate her reasons, maybe she would find the underlying cause for this desire.

"I want to find a loving partner."

What for?

"I have an empty feeling, a feeling of lack inside. I want a partner so that I can fill that void and feel complete."

Ok, this was quite easy. But what if we exchange "I want a loving partner" for "I want a new flashy car," or "I want to achieve professional success"?

What for?

"I feel a sense of lack. I want a new flashy car so that I can get the approval of other people. That car is a symbol of money and success, and people will like me, respect me, and look up to me if I have one."

Why do you want the approval of other people?

"I feel like I'm not enough. If others approve of me, I approve of me. I need the validation to feel good."

So do you want the approval of other people, or do you want to feel good and complete?"

"I want to feel good and complete. Deep down, I am insecure."

Do you need the approval of other people to feel good, secure, and complete?

"I guess so…"

I bet you're not seeking everyone's approval. You're not seeking the Dalai Lama's approval. You're seeking your peers' approval, and that of people you believe have some degree of authority.

"Yes, that's correct."

You've been led to believe that by being approved of by someone you consider to be more worthy than you, your worth will increase—and thus you will feel happier and more complete. Do you see the fallacy in this? You give others more worth than you give yourself, and then you need those very same people to give you your worth back so that you can feel worthy. They have the power. Yet it was you who gave them the power—so who's got the power after all?

There's always a reason for wanting whatever it is that we want, and if we go deeply into the "why," it will always end up being about happiness and completeness. This is a recurrent theme in this book and in all genuine spiritual books.

Spirituality is about ending the feeling of lack, which means we have to be everything. If we are everything, we can't feel that we lack anything. To be everything, we have to stop being something. To be the Whole, we have to stop being a "part"—"I." By breaking the harsh barriers of this physical body through spiritual practice, our awareness "expands[7]" from a localized spot to a non-localized awareness. When

---

[7] It doesn't actually expand or change, but it may feel like it. It's like breaking a pot—the space inside the pot doesn't change or expand into the outside space; it has always been one with it. It's just that the pot gave the illusion of separation.

there's no location, our circumference is everywhere, but our center is—nowhere.

This pursuit of security, of feeling good, of being happy, of being totally contented and complete is the highest pursuit. It's seeking God.

God is absolute happiness. God is peace and bliss beyond comprehension. That's the goal of humanity, that's your goal—to be perpetually happy, to be blissful beyond any possible understanding. That is being one with God, which is the purpose of all Yogas and genuine spirituality.

All unhappiness comes from unfulfilled desire. When we find our true nature, when we find God, the ultimate desire for happiness and completeness is fulfilled, and therefore, we will no longer be unhappy. That is real Freedom.

If you understand that what you want is to be happy, and that the only reason you want to achieve whatever it is that you want to achieve (e.g., mundane success, acquiring new possessions, or any other externally-oriented goal) is because you believe these things will bring you happiness, then you will not desire them anymore. You will only wish for absolute happiness, absolute bliss, absolute peace, and absolute ecstasy. You don't need "things" as the intermediary of happiness—they are a very poor middleman anyway. If you want happiness and completeness, things are but a scam. What you really want is the end of all desires—the desirelessness that comes with realizing your true blissful nature.

Desires = restlessness.

Desireless = peacefulness.

> "God is absolute bliss."
>
> - ATHARVA VEDA

Few have the genuine desire to realize the highest truth, and fewer still have the self-sincerity, discipline, and patience to attain it. This is exclusively a result of their lack of discernment. They are also looking for that supreme happiness, and think a "successful life" (whatever "successful" may mean to them in terms of achievements in society) or acquiring material wealth will bring it.

But you are not going to settle for a temporarily successful life. You are going for the eternal. This is the reason you are reading this book and why you do spiritual practice. You want to be eternally happy.

Why would you want to achieve any lesser goals than this unbounded bliss? Understanding this gives rise to total abstention from greed (*Aparigraha*).

Of course some bad habits may still emerge from time to time; of course your desires for material things may still pop up from time to time; but neither will fool you anymore because you know that none of these things will ultimately satisfy you. It's smoke from a smoldering—and about to be extinguished—fire.

With time, practice, and surrender, there will come a day when no more desires for these types of things emerge anymore. When that day comes, you shall be ready for the beginning of true "non-possessiveness" (Aparigraha). And you'll realize that you don't even really possess your "I"—it belongs to the universal dance of God. That's the ultimate form of *Aparigraha*.

Your Mind is the Ruler of Value

I want you to notice that whatever you see, it actually doesn't mean anything in itself. It is your own mind that applies an interpretation to what you are perceiving.

We give meaning to everything we perceive.

Your thoughts and constant interpretations color whatever you perceive, and attribute a meaning to it in accordance to your "self." Everything we apprehend is automatically perceived in a way that is either beneficial or harmful to our survival and self-continuance (both of the body and of our identity).

Imagine that your grandmother gave you an old family bracelet moments before her death, and whispered to you "This bracelet has been with our family for five generations. Keep it safe. This is my last wish."

The bracelet now carries with it a powerful emotional charge. It may be totally meaningless to everyone else, but to you—it is exceptionally important.

A few weeks later, at a friends' reunion, you bring that bracelet and show it to your friends. Suddenly, a friend says that she has a similar bracelet. She takes it off of her arm and asks you to hand yours to her so that she can compare how similar they are. Lo and behold, the bracelets are identical! Your friend can't pinpoint any difference between them.

Accidentally, she drops both, and after picking them up, you are horrified. Now, you don't know which bracelet is yours and which bracelet is your friend's! "Don't worry, they are exactly the same," says your friend. "You don't understand; this bracelet is special! It was given to me by my grandmother right before she passed away," you reply.

But how could you even tell the difference between them? You can't!

You see, *it's not the object in itself, but the meaning and value we ascribe to it that makes it meaningful and valuable.*

Hence we must understand that *we give everything we perceive all the value that it has for us.* We can realize that nothing has value in and of itself, but only if we venture beyond our usual limiting mind.

To perceive something as it really is, you need to distill all coloration from your awareness.

If you are looking at everything with glasses that have purple hued lenses, you'd think that everything is purplish. It is not.

Look at whatever you see during your day and realize that

nothing has value or meaning in itself—things are intrinsically empty. Pay close attention to those things that you feel especially attached or attracted to. You will soon find out, experientially, that there's no more useless and nonsensical obsession than pursuing happiness and fulfillment through materiality.

Our current culture has distorted the way we perceive this world. If I asked you to think of something extremely valuable to you right now, I bet you wouldn't think about water. Yet water is one of the most valuable things a human being can have. But we take it for granted.

Do you know what else we take for granted?

Our own consciousness.

Don't take it for granted. Pay attention to it. It is calling you! Without consciousness, nothing would be.

Consciousness is our mother—and our father. And we, as consciousness, are its child. Self-recognizing oneself to be this consciousness is the most valuable achievement in the whole universe.

CHAPTER 6

SAUCA
THE WHOLE-BEING DETOX

Sauca denotes purity of body and mind. It means "purity" or "cleanliness." When this Niyama was first written around 15 centuries ago in ancient rural India, people used to "purify" their bodies with water, clay, cow pats, and cow urine. This is not applicable today for obvious reasons.

So rather than commenting on the ancient ways, let's take this understanding to a more contemporary setting so that we can truly cleanse our bodies, actions, and mind.

Taking good care of the body is important, so this is where we will begin.

> "To keep the body in good health is a duty... otherwise we shall not be able to keep our mind strong and clear."
>
> - THE BUDDHA

THE IMPORTANCE OF TAKING GOOD CARE OF THE BODY

When we think about taking care of the body in our spiritual journey, one of the first things that comes to mind is food.

The best diet in terms of spiritual purposes always depends on the individual. Generally, moderate consumption of vegetarian food (or plant-based), adequate and consistent sleep, and a mixture of stretching, aerobic (cardiovascular), and anaerobic (e.g., weightlifting) exercises will put you in the best possible physical condition. These, together with proper meditation (which promotes calmness and decreases stress), are the perfect combination. But, although we may already know this conceptually, it takes a powerful mindset to propel us to actually take consistent action.

Upon reaching a deep level of purification, the mind matures into quietness and delicacy, and an innate intelligence emerges from within. It is this intelligence that dictates the most accurate type of food for the spiritual seeker.

The well-being of our body has an immediate influence on our nadis and on the flow of life-force through them. A healthier physical body serves as the basis for a powerful cultivation, preservation, circulation, and transmutation of energy.

Rather than rejecting the body, we should embrace it as our vehicle of expression in this relative world. This acceptance prevents many conflicts or inner turmoil that may emerge during our path, and also saves us from many of the pitfalls associated with such rejection. A fragmented expression of being is not a proper instrument of the divine in this relative world; after all, the body is also the Self—it's all one single Reality.

In spirituality, lots of seekers neglect their body and its health. "I'm not my body" or "I don't care about what happens to the body" are sentences we frequently hear. Now, I'm not saying that these sentences are not true, but they more often than not come from an ego-based position. Being exceedingly attached to the body or not caring about it are not proper ways of treading our spiritual path. These kinds of extremes should be avoided. Both of them are a manifestation of imbalance.

Forming an appropriate and well-adjusted relationship with our body is important because the body is our vehicle of expression in this physical world. Having it in good physical condition while maintaining proper health are requirements that assure your bodily system will be able to do whatever it is supposed to do in this world.

Being too attached to it is a clear sign of ignorance because regardless of what lengths you go to take care of it (often becoming an obsession), eventually it will become sick and die. Wasting so much time taking care of and improving something that is temporary is an unconscious behavior driven by self-survival.

On the other hand, spiritual seekers in particular like to dwell in "spaced out" states not caring about their bodies at all, neglecting proper nutrition, exercise, and flexibility.

With that being said, the majority of people are not overly attached to their body in the sense of being obsessive about its health and fitness; more of them fall into the category of unconsciously mistreating it. This means feeding it with unhealthy food, developing bad posture, smoking, drinking alcohol, taking drugs, being weak, not exercising, or not having any kind of flexibility.

All of these unconscious behaviors and habits can be overcome through mindfulness and spiritual practice, although not without a fight. You have the power to take conscious control of all these unconscious aspects in your life, and can fine-tune them to be more in harmony and more predisposed to spiritual practice and to the overall spiritual journey.

Why not start today?

In today's world, austerity is not the way. If you wreck your health, you will lack the endurance, energy, vitality, motivation, and self-control to go all the way. On the other hand, indulgence is not the way either—that's akin to destroying your mental discipline, stamina, and power of will.

Despite what many may think, spirituality is not only about the mind or spirit—it is also a precious tool that promotes a wholesome relationship with the body. Meditation/spiritual practice has a soothing effect on the body, improving its health. Even the scientific community (which is based heavily in materialism) has embraced meditation, empirically claiming that those who practice it have less risk of heart attacks and strokes, lower blood pressure, reduced ADHD symptoms, less chronic pain, etc.

Besides our body, the way we approach our interaction with others throughout our spiritual journey is also of utmost importance. That's what we'll tackle next.

Interaction With Others in our Spiritual Journey

As you progress on your spiritual journey, you may become more sensitive or vulnerable. As you open to your own inner being and begin to surrender your ego-self, hanging around unconscious people may be tough. You may have difficulty relating to them, similar to what might happen if a classical music fan mistakenly entered a heavy metal concert. This is not a suggestion to avoid, ignore or retreat from the physical world, or to avoid socializing, but rather a word of caution to help prevent your mind from being corrupted by spiritually immature people.

The energy of unconscious and insensitive beings will probably cause you some trouble. My advice is to be as real and authentic as possible. By this I mean, don't try to please others by saying things that they want to hear, don't nod your head in agreement if you don't agree with them, and don't be afraid to mention how your point of view is different from theirs (and probably deeper). Don't be fake, hollow, or have totally meaningless conversations. Otherwise, it will cause the mind-purification process you've been working on in your spiritual journey to significantly regress, and it will hinder your ability to practice what is shared in this book, especially considering that these practices require a still mind that is free of pollution and negative energy and harmful influences.

By staying real to yourself, you may be doing these people a great favor by elevating them into a level of awareness, knowledge, and lucidity that they have never experienced before. They may be perplexed or shocked by hearing your words. Wow! Perhaps they've never dreamed that behind your eyes lay something so deep or so profound.

Or they may laugh at or ridicule you, and point out how wrong you are. It's okay—you can't show the color yellow to a blind person. Not everyone is meant to awaken; not everyone is ready to awaken; not everyone will awaken.

You must use your discernment and listen to your heart, though. Don't try to teach anyone or show how wrong they are; don't behave like you're the "wise one" and they are just "ignorant." Never let the ego use what is written in this chapter to its benefit. Just be real to yourself and let the light from within shine to the best of your ability. This too is a great purification.

Before realizing your true inherent nature of bliss, or even before being able to awaken profound insight and direct experiences into the nature of the cosmos, your humor, mood, and lucidity level can quickly be disturbed by the world and by "ignorant," "negative," or "non-spiritual" people. When you interact with such beings, if they carry "low-quality" thoughts (which often end up translated into words), their low vibration and subtle energetic emanations may disrupt the clarity and mindfulness of your current "level" of consciousness, making you temporarily operate below it. This will happen if you haven't fully stabilized and integrated this higher mode of functioning.

Nonetheless, it's like olive oil entering into a glass of crystalline water—at first it will seem to have blended together (their energy affects you) but as soon as you get back on your feet ("recover" lucidity, or are more spiritually mature), you will see how both of your energies just cannot blend.

Afterward, looking back, you will think, "Why did I react that way?", or "How come I said so and so?" It's okay. As soon as you resume your base level of consciousness, you will become aware of what happened, and thus you strengthen your level of clarity and mindfulness, thereby preventing it from happening again with such ease (or at all).

Once you are spiritually mature enough, you will no longer be affected by external influences from the dimension of ignorance.

If someone is trying to stop smoking, they should not be

hanging out with other smokers—that will just make the whole process harder (in addition to reaping terrible health repercussions by indirectly inhaling the smoke). But as soon as someone successfully quits smoking, then there's no problem whatsoever hanging out with smokers and giving them their space to smoke in a way that the non-smoker doesn't end up inhaling it.

Perhaps, led by example, some will decide to stop smoking as well, following healthier footsteps! Leaving the smoky ignorance of Maya behind, they may use your footsteps as a lighthouse, illuminating the journey back to their original essence.

This Niyama of purity, however, goes way beyond the body and our relationships. It also concerns purity of mind. This inner purity requires an inner cleanse—it is a byproduct of our spiritual practices.

INNER CLEANSE

You must genuinely understand that solutions to inner problems are not found through external means.

If somebody were to attack your physical body, you would defend yourself.

If someone or some situation were to attack your "inner self" (i.e., your conceptual self, the idea you have about who you are, your identity), then how could you defend yourself? Certainly not in the same way. To combat this, you develop defense mechanisms that attempt to protect your "self" from further attacks/suffering, by hiding it behind masks and conditioning. But these defense mechanisms also prevent you from truly living life to its fullest, because they limit and shape the way you behave, think, speak, and live.

Defense mechanisms come in a variety of shapes and sizes, and they are deeply engrained in our personality structure, extending beyond the typical example of a person who is arrogant (or shy, timid, stubborn, etc.), but doesn't know that such a personality-facet is just a mask to hide their profound sadness, fragility, and loneliness from themselves and others.

For example, let's suppose that a man named Oscar always

had long and beautiful hair as a child and teenager. However, as he became older, he started losing some hair, and eventually he had to have a buzz cut. In truth, most people thought Oscar looked great with this new style, but he felt terrible.

When he was young, his father—who was bald—was slightly abusive and was constantly fighting with Oscar's mother. Oscar often overheard his mother scream "I hate you" to his father, and he felt terribly sad. This made him subconsciously attribute his father's look (bald) to sorrow and with something bad.

This is why he was so proud of his beautiful long hair, because it was a statement that he was "different" from his father. Long hair was a defense mechanism used by Oscar to keep sorrow and pain away. Then, when Oscar became older and had to have a buzz cut, he became depressed. Not because he had no hair, but because it reminded him of his father, although this connection was not something that he was consciously aware of.

As time went by, Oscar sought out new hair treatments including transplants, and toupees. Because he thought his problem was a physical one (lack of hair), he reasoned that the solution would also be a physical one (having the hair back). He ended up getting a hair transplant and he felt amazing again.

But getting his hair back did not fix the underlying problem—it only masked and buried it. This was a defense mechanism that Oscar unconsciously created due to psychological trauma. And just like we cannot comb our hair in its mirror reflection, we cannot fix an internal issue by making an external correction—which is what Oscar did.

When Oscar practices deep meditation, he will be confronted with his past, sorrow, trauma, his clinging to his hair as a form of "sorrow-protection," and so on. He then must realize that all of that is just a temporary facet of an ephemeral identity ("Oscar"), and not who he truly is (pure Consciousness with no trauma, sorrow, past, future, or any facets at all for that matter).

With this being said, I want you to identify some problem that you have deep down, some trauma or something that *you aware of*, but you pretend that you are not. You hide it or push it away every time it pops up, or you try not to think about it. It is something that, although it has roots deep down in the subconscious mind, there are always weeds surfacing every now and then.

Try to identify it right now. Even if you can't identify any specific issue at this moment, it will pop up sooner or later (keep the mental intention to become extremely alert once that issue pops up).

As soon as that problem that you've been ignoring surfaces, I want you to notice what is it that hurts. What kind of physical sensations are you experiencing? Why are they bad? Does your heart feel heavy? Does your mind rush with thoughts and imagery? When that happens, stop for a moment and do your best to impersonally watch these raw feelings, emotions, and thoughts. Notice that they are not bad in and of themselves; they are just sensations, interpretations, and concepts. Don't back off. Stay with the rawness of the situation—witness it without letting yourself be enveloped by it.

Dig deep down into the root of that trauma or issue and find out where it all started. Find the underlying causes. When you get to the source of something and are able to impersonally observe the raw emotions, feelings, and thoughts that occur, *without identifying y*ourself with them, these issues lose their power. A higher state of consciousness emerges that allows you to comprehend them better and let them go; you experience a powerful emptiness that releases your attachment to those traumas.

If you keep resisting them, they shall persist, but once you comprehend them and allow them to be there without judging, just impersonally feeling their raw sensations (or whatever they bring up at that moment), they will lose their energy—which comes from you—and eventually disappear. This is really important, and it can help you overcome any stumbling block that you may experience in your sadhana.

Through this simple yet deep process, which requires some maturity and discernment that only come with consistent meditation, you can purify your mind in a fashion similar to what happens during profound meditation, but more quickly. After all, such introspection is indeed already a profound meditation in itself.

The Pragmatic Extermination of Beliefs

Beliefs can be very powerful. Many people would be willing to die for what they believe, even though that doesn't make those beliefs any truer.

In spirituality, beliefs can be a plague—they will corrupt your discernment and perspective, and if you allow them to grow, they can take over your life. If you are on a genuine spiritual journey, dismantling all of your beliefs will sooner or later become critical.

There is a difference between *truly* knowing something versus just believing it. The first comes from directly experiencing that "something," while the second comes from second-hand knowledge (something you heard, read, etc.).

Let's analyze your spiritual beliefs. This will work as a powerful "*Sauca* (purification) of mind."

You can begin by taking a piece of paper and writing them down (you can write on your computer or smartphone, but pen and paper are preferable because they create a more intimate experience). Then, look at each belief and ask yourself:

How do I know that? From reading and hearing, or from direct experience?

If it's not from direct experience, discard that belief immediately. Your spiritual foundation must be based on the truth, not on lies—you want to have a clean slate.

This may not be easy to do, because your ego-mind may trick you into believing that you have no beliefs, or perhaps, it's just that right now you can't seem to recognize any spiritual beliefs that you might have. So, to go further into this matter, let's take ten common spiritual dictums and break them down. This will help you assess whether you have some of these spiritual beliefs or not. Keep in mind that you should employ the same line of questioning that you did before.

Let's start with:

1) "I am pure Consciousness/God/Spirit/Self."

How do you know that?

From reading, or from experience?

Is this sentence true for you? Be honest.

(repeat these questions to all the following sentences)

2) "The whole Universe is in me."

3) "This world is but a dream."

4) "In essence, I am not my body."

5) "In essence, I am not my mind."

6) "I am not a separate self."

7) "Acquiring material wealth doesn't provide lasting happiness and peace."

8) "The chakras are as real as my body."

9) "It is possible to end all suffering and misery."

10) "My natural state is one of pure peace and bliss."

Be real. If you've answered five or more of these questions from "direct experience," then you are doing great. If below five, no problem, you'll get there eventually; just continue to put the required time and effort into your spiritual practice.

If you've answered all ten in the positive, I congratulate you.

Nonetheless, let's explore what is real for everyone reading this book who has not yet realize their true nature. These are not beliefs, they are factual and will likely parallel your own current direct experience:

1) "Currently, I am not fully satisfied."

2) "What I have done thus far in my life has not brought lasting satisfaction."

3) "I am seeking something."

4) "I am seeking happiness, peace, and completeness."

5) "I don't know."

These are very real. Rather than believing in something that you have not experienced, make sure that you take what's real in your current direct experience and use it to grow your understanding and motivation to go further into realizing whether these previous ten spiritual dictums (or any others for that matter) are true or not.

Let's see:

1) "Currently, I am not fully satisfied."

A fully satisfied being seeks nothing, desires nothing, wants nothing. He or she is at total peace, totally fulfilled. That human being just is.

If one is not fully satisfied, one must look out for what is missing. What is missing? What would make you fully satisfied?

Which leads us into the second:

2) "What I have done thus far in my life has not brought lasting satisfaction."

You may not know if a thing such as lasting satisfaction even exists. What most people have done in their life may bring *some* satisfaction, but it doesn't last. Why are you reading this book? You may have had a glimpse of the eternity of completeness—and you want more of that. The contentment of life is not found in the contents of life but in living life as Life with a capital L, which is another name for the true Self. It's not in anything specific in life but when there are no boundaries between you and life—between you and whatever is happening.

People say that it's the little moments in life that bring the most joy because in those very moments, they are present, out of their heads, in the *now*. When they are in the present moment, their limiting boundaries diminish, allowing them to enjoy the beautiful tapestry of life. This is a glimpse of living life as Life with a capital L.

When you witness greatness, for a short instant you become greatness. You and that greatness lose separation, and both are One. It's freeing! In awe, you disappear. When the illusion of being a separate identity disappears, God flashes His nature of bliss.

You seek greatness! Greatness is when the ego is no more. Though greatness can present itself in many forms, its essence is one of no-mind unity. This is what spirituality brings to the table: the ultimate form of Greatness. That's what you seek, and what will finally bring ever-lasting satisfaction.

Hence 3) & 4), "I am seeking something," and "I am seeking happiness, peace, and completeness."

Which brings us to 5) "I don't know."

Realizing and admitting that you don't know opens space in your mind to receive pointers and instructions that will show you the way in to the soul of Being. To leap beyond what is currently known (which is not sufficient, otherwise one would not be seeking enlightenment), one needs the humility and discernment to internally allow a "space of not-knowing." This not-knowing is not ignorance, but rather is the first step towards *true knowledge.* Insight doesn't "occur" when the mind is full—it occurs when the mind is empty.

Beliefs are like clouds that prevent you from seeing the sunlight. Questioning and cleansing your mind of beliefs is akin to dissipating those clouds and allowing the sun to shine through the empty sky! Oh, what a beautiful day that is.

CHAPTER 7

SANTOSA
THE VIRTUOSITY OF CONTENTMENT

"Whatever happiness there may be in enjoyment in this world, and whatever greater happiness there may be in the celestial world, they do not amount to one sixteenth of the happiness attained from the cessation of desire"

- VYASA'S COMMENTARY ON THE YOGA SUTRAS

Santosa is the second Niyama, and it is a Sanskrit word that comes from the roots *sam* (altogether, totally, completely; the same "sam" as in *samadhi*) and *tosa* (contentment, satisfaction). It can be translated as complete contentment, total delight, utter gratification, and so on.

When we search for contentment or satisfaction in this world, can we find it? Yes. Let me tell you when: when you fulfill a desire.

Think of something that you really wanted, something that you pursued and that you finally achieved at some point. At the precise moment when you achieved it, you experienced complete contentment, total satisfaction, utter delight.

But it was short-lived. That contentment may have lasted for a few seconds, minutes, hours, days, weeks, or months, but then it faded. Then you chose a new goal, a new desire that you began pursuing. This goes on and on until you finally arrive at the ultimate desire: ending all desires so that you can be ever-happy. In order to achieve this, you explore meditation, dive into spirituality, and seek enlightenment. That's why you're reading this book right now!

But what I want to show you with this whole book is that perpetual contentment already lies within you—you are just unaware of it. This is not fancy New-Age self-help rubbish talk; it's really true.

If you didn't already have perpetual contentment within you, if it weren't already present but just apparently obfuscated, then this would mean that you could potentially gain it, which would also mean that you could lose it. And if you could lose it, then it would not be worth it.

Perpetual contentment must be something that is already present at all times, rather than something to be gained, otherwise enlightenment, which is the goal of all authentic spirituality, would not be more valuable than any other ephemeral thing.

You are breathing at all times, but you are not aware of it, are you? Now as you read this, you'll probably become aware of the air flowing in and going out. It was already present but you just weren't paying attention to it. In the same way, we have so much stuff blocking the flow of contentment from within (i.e., desires) that only when what is causing a blockage stops blocking (i.e., desire is fulfilled) do we allow ourselves to experience that tasty joy of pure contentment. But it was there all along.

So, what would it be like when there are no more desires? Let us get a little taste of it:

Imagine that for some reason, you haven't seen the person you absolutely love the most in over a year. Imagine the built-up desire and the subsequent release of tension when you are finally with that person again. At that moment, your intense longing to be together is fulfilled; at that moment, you are desireless—you are drinking the joy of pure contentment[8].

---

[8] Alternatively, instead of being to a person that you love, you can apply this to something that you've always wanted to do or to get, but that you've never been able to. The built-up desire and subsequent release of tension when you finally achieve it will be similar.

Now, magically expand that finite moment into perpetuity. That's perpetual contentment!

Now here comes the kicker: with perpetual contentment, the body-mind won't have any purpose or motivation to do anything at all—there's just no will toward any "movement" within this dual world because there is perfect unbroken fulfillment. In such a state, the bliss is perpetuated not only in the mind but also in the senses and the body. Everything is simply this pure bliss. Body and mind are partially active in such a state, but it is difficult to perform activities or do anything because the bliss has become too strong to allow engagement with normal daily living.

So how can we reconcile this?

There's one thing above all others with which your relative expression naturally aligns. Typically, it is something that allows your creativity to come through, but ultimately, it's something that causes an impact in the world, regardless of the scale of such actions. What this means is that by performing this activity, you are expressing the light of awareness through those actions—whatever they may be.

That's what will create a habit that will anchor your consciousness to the body and allow it to keep functioning in the world, while continuously bathing in contentment, joy, and pleasure. It's as if your relative expression was supposed to do exactly that in this world. This is something that your own path will show you—nobody can choose it for you.

It is the love to continuously perform that activity that will help you to maintain a grounded "transcendental-I[9]."

It is curious to realize that even though the spiritual path will show you that nothing has any meaning in and of itself, it will also enable you to discover and actualize your relative purpose in this world. These are not separate things, but rather a different manifestation of the same inherent divinity!

---

[9] The pure "I;" The enlightened "I" that does not perceive anything as separated from itself. The residue of a seemingly relative consciousness that remains in enlightened beings after they realize their true egoless nature so that they can live and operate in the world.

AM I IN CONTROL?

Santosa is also about letting go of the illusion of control. Allowing what is, without rejecting it, is contentment.

If you reject something, you are suffering. If you allow it without embracing it, you don't suffer. This doesn't mean that the situation in question cannot change, or that you shouldn't do anything to change it, or that you should be happy with mediocrity. What it does mean is that you don't resist the situation, and therefore your inner state is not perturbed by it. This allows mindfulness and calmness to permeate through the situation, enabling you to see and deal with it from a higher perspective.

For example, if you find out that you have a terminal disease, allowing something doesn't mean that you give up all hope, resign yourself to it and just allow your body to deteriorate and die, evoking "karma" or "God's will" as reasons. No. You can't possibly know if overcoming such a disease is part of your life's path and karma, or not.

What this means is that you accept that you do have such a condition (i.e., accepting the now, allowing what is already present rather than denying and suppressing it), and then you look for possible solutions and for the best path to treat the illness.

The idea of having no control of, or being powerless over your life and what course it will follow may be too much for most people. They may feel desperate that things are out of their hands. And when helplessness arises, misery is its closest companion.

The fact of the matter is that you are not in control of your life and its path. Realizing this insight through direct experience is essential. Let's see:

Did you consciously choose to be born to your parents? Forget those who affirm, "I, as a soul, have chosen my birth parents because being born into that family created the best possibilities for me to experience my karma and fulfill my worldly purpose." I'm not questioning whether such an affirmation is true or false—it's just that you, the person who is reading this book right now and who is looking for enlightenment, certainly didn't choose such.

Did you ever choose to be in a traffic jam?

Did you ever choose to be rejected or to be told no?

I could give innumerable examples, but it's easy to see that if you were truly in control of your life, you would never experience suffering. No one in their right mind would ever suffer on purpose, and if you were in control, you'd always be totally happy.

So, you are not really in control. You can do your best to go in the direction that you perceive your interests to be, but whether that works out or not, it's not really up to you.

We have all heard that the Harry Potter books were rejected over and over again more than ten times before finally being accepted by a publisher, and then subsequently, becoming the best-selling book series of all time.

We have all heard about those who said: "I got so many no's, but I kept on trying until I got a yes, and thus fulfilled my dream."

Were those people in control? Obviously not, otherwise they would haven't gotten a "no" in the first place. But something in them made them persist, and eventually, they did it (i.e., gained recognition from society). That was supposed to happen. But it doesn't happen all the time.

How many people try their hardest, but fail to get such recognition? Sometimes, they get it after they die, such as Galileo Galilei[10] or Vincent van Gogh[11], who are just some

---

[10] Often called the "father of observational astronomy," he was sentenced to life imprisonment by the Church.

[11] He had no success, and due to mental illness and poverty, committed suicide at 37 years old. Nowadays, his paintings sell for millions of dollars; and he even had a painting sell for more than $80 million.

famous names that only received proper recognition posthumously. But many died without "fulfilling their dreams" despite working hard to achieve them. We never hear about those.

When I first wrote *Kriya Yoga Exposed*, I had no idea whether anyone would read it or not. I had no idea where all of this was going. I didn't know, at the time, that I would write and publish more books. I didn't know whether that very first book would change anyone's life. And you know what? I was already satisfied and happy even before writing it (that's why it was written in the first place, from the heart), and whatever ensued from that, so be it.

What I want to convey through this is that contentment must not be dependent on whether we get what we want, be this "things," recognition, appreciation, or even love.

Total contentment or perfect satisfaction must come from within, from the very core of consciousness. It comes from desirelessness. That's the sacred jewel of Santosa.

From Drifting to Controlling to Dancing

There are three main levels of realization (or lack of it) concerning "control":

1) Ignorant Ego

I'm at the mercy of life and its events. I can't control anything; I can't design my life the way I want it. It's totally out of my control. I abide in mediocrity.

2) Smart Ego

I'm in control of my life. I can design it the way I want; though there may be obstacles, ultimately, I am the architect of my path. I am or will be a success.

3) Spiritual Seeker

I am not in control of my life in the grand scheme of things. I can control some decisions, but not all of them. I will do the best I can to be in harmony with life and the universe.

4) Enlightened Being

I am one with Life. As the stream of life flows, so I flow. I am not at the mercy of life, nor can I control it—because I am it. I go with it, as it.

Which level are you at? Can you make a jump to the next level?

The first level doesn't require anything—it's the default level of human beings.

The second level requires self-development—it's what the majority of self-help, "life coaches," Neuro-linguistic programming and self-improvement courses, and most meditation teachers instruct. Success is equated with recognition in society, often financially and in social status.

The third level begins after self-development because it's self-transcendence. If you are reading this book, then there's a high probability that you are already at this level.

After realizing through discernment and spiritual practice that the "self" is an ephemeral play in the screen of consciousness, a temporary false subject, and an illusion without inherent existence in itself, the mature spiritual seeker becomes aware of the fact that improving or developing it won't cease its suffering nor help it to achieve eternal happiness and fulfillment. In other words, since the "self" is nothing more than an agglomerate of thoughts, feelings, perceptions, and sensations, it's but a passing wind on the eternal sky of consciousness (that which witnesses thoughts, feelings, perceptions, and sensations—but is none of them).

Eternal life can only be found in what is not temporary— which is pure consciousness, the true Self. That's where mature spiritual seekers focus and abide by, in their own background of awareness, trying their best to dance with life. That's the bridge toward the fourth and final level.

So here's how things may stand for you right now:

You might say that although there are countless events and happenings outside of your control, you, as an apparent individual entity, definitely seem to have a choice in a variety of personal decisions throughout each day (you still have the sense of being the doer of actions or the decider of choices). For example, you may think that getting this book and reading it was your own decision.

If this is the case (appearing that you still have some power of choice), you should always decide according to what you feel is best to "advance" in your spiritual journey. This will prevent the creation of new barriers or obstacles in your spiritual practice (often called "karma"). This book was mostly written with the consideration that you reside in this "zone" of semi-free choice, and so it's meant to help you aim your decisions toward the spiritual summit of Self-Realization.

Even if we were to say that everything is predestined, certainly you cannot know what is in store for you. Thus, it still seems to be up to you to decide whatever you wish to choose. So you make the best possible decision according to your current level of wisdom and intuition. And because you have infinite possibilities of choice in every moment of your life, what you decide to do is of extreme importance.

If you lack the lucidity to act consciously, your acts and outcomes will be unconscious—they will be the result of mere past conditioning. Many people make choices that they don't even recognize as "choices," simply because such choices were made in total unawareness, and hence seem to be a byproduct of randomness or of the "environment" ("Ignorant Ego").

This failure to take responsibility for one's own choices can cause great harm when one is on a profound and authentic spiritual journey. To fight this off and break the current cycle one might be trapped in, it is imperative to begin acting from a higher state of consciousness.

As you shift to a higher level of consciousness, you become more capable of using your apparent free will and making fully conscious choices.

Being present can function as portal to this higher state of consciousness:

Relax. Take a deep breath. Look around. Feel your sense of being present. Are you present right now? Yes? Take your time.

* * *

Take another deep breath. Relax some more. At this moment, if just for a single minute, allow yourself to be at peace. Allow yourself to be content with what is currently present within the space of your awareness. What's missing? Don't use the mind to answer it. Stay present.

In this very moment, whenever you are totally present, if just for a brief second, you are totally content. Being in the present moment is Santosa.

CHAPTER **8**

TAPAS
THE ART OF EGG HATCHING

Tapas is quite an interesting Niyama. It is normally understood as "austerity," yet if we go to the root of the word we'll see a deeper story. First and foremost, take all of the aspects of it that recommend body mortification and the typical ridiculous austerities and put them in the trash, because they won't take you anywhere but toward misery. Don't give any thought or credence to this type of "tapas."

Tap means "to burn" or "to heat," and Tapas can itself be seen as "fire" or "heat." Fire, as you can probably guess, is intimately related to Kundalini energy.

Through Kundalini Yoga, Kriya Yoga, and other spiritual disciplines, the inner fire (Kundalini) is awakened[12]. This is

---

[12] If you perform the technique of Kriya Supreme Fire, for example, you will feel immense heat in your belly-area, spreading through your whole body. This is a consequence of the process and the awakening of Kundalini.

Tapas—hence why it's also called meditation, the art of "egg hatching." In other words, it's the incubation of your attention on your inner world with the purpose of awakening the Kundalini (fire) and giving birth to the realization of being God, the infinite consciousness.

Tapas is, therefore, synonymous with spiritual practice, which is the crux of all spiritual work. If you don't practice, you're not going anywhere. Whenever you do spiritual practice, you are cleaning both the conscious and the subconscious mind by increasing the power of your life-force, discernment, understanding, quietness, concentration, mindfulness, clarity, awareness, and boosting your yearning for enlightenment.

Intellectual spiritual understanding is a good beginning, but if you don't put instructions and theory into action, then you're merely playing make-believe. You must also consciously infuse spirituality into your whole life. A seeker can't expect to practice for one hour per day (sitting practice), sleep for 6 to 8 hours, and then spend the rest of the time engrossed in the world without any lucidity, just being his "old self." Not that there's a "new self" that we want to reach, but it is a fact that when you make the switch from a non-seeker (i.e., someone totally uninterested in spiritual or self-transcendence endeavors or someone who lives their life without ever looking within or giving a second thought to what is real, life, consciousness, or God) to a genuine seeker (i.e., when you realize that enlightenment, Self-realization, God, Buddha-nature, etc., is what you truly want), there are certain aspects, qualities, and characteristics that emerge in you, such as a sudden dispassion toward superficial things, increased interest in all spiritual matters, a heightened sense of introspection, and a strength to face one's own beliefs, trauma, etc. In addition, some spiritual books like this one help to awaken the required discernment[13] by shedding light onto your understanding, providing deep insight and "aha" moments.

The more you practice Yogic (e.g., *Kriya Pranayama*, *Kriya Supreme Fire*), Buddhist (e.g., *Anapanasati*, *Tummo*), nondual (e.g., *Self-Inquiry*, *Shikantaza*), or any other type of spiritual practice, the more your mind will be focused and silent throughout the day, and the more you'll get used to and actually value inner silence and lucidity.

---

[13] All kinds of discernment are important. Starting with the discrimination between the subject (you, the experiencer, awareness) and objects (the contents of the mind, movements of awareness), followed by the discrimination between real, pure teachings and fake, dogmatic teachings, and so on.

Spiritual Practice is the Golden Shining Jewel

Meditation is the art and process of realizing our inherent unity with the Cosmos—our non-separateness.

Meditation, spiritual practice or *sadhana* is the ultimate form of activity. The majority of your spiritual progress is achieved through your efforts in sitting meditation and its after-state that is applied and integrated throughout your daily life, constantly upgrading the "base level" of your relative consciousness[14].

The necessary insight, discernment, and maturity to reach your true potential and realize your unlimited nature are outcomes of a proper and diligent spiritual practice or meditation[15].

Meditation, however, is a term that is poorly understood. There are countless definitions, some more concrete, while others are entirely abstract and ambiguous. Its meaning is also dependent upon whichever tradition we're studying,

---

[14] As you get deeper into the purification of your mind, old negative patterns start to erode, deprogramming the behaviors, actions, decisions, etc., that are not conducive to enlightenment.

[15] Although this can also happen just by reading or hearing a powerful instruction given by an awakened guru (or in his/her presence), though it probably means that the seeker did spiritual practice in a previous life.

because different traditions have ascribed different meanings to what western languages such as English have translated as *meditation*[16].

To make sure it is clear, whenever the terms spiritual practice or meditation are used in this book, they mean: *the employment of our body, mind, and awareness in a methodical and practical manner for the purpose of achieving a deeper state of consciousness that allows one to gain insight into and then abide as one's essence.*

Spiritual practice is the endeavor of finding out who we truly are. We are using our individual consciousness to go beyond its narrow field of awareness into a broader and more expansive universal awareness. In other words, we are attempting to go from being a person (limited individual consciousness) to being God (unlimited universal consciousness).

Our individual consciousness, descending from the universal field of consciousness where everything lies in potential, manifests itself via the life force (prana) which runs through our energy body by virtue of the nervous system (or nadis), passing through the seven main chakras (the main plexuses).

---

[16] In the famous Yoga Sutras of Patanjali, *dhyana* has been translated as *meditation*.

Imprisoned in the body, consciousness becomes identified with its limited physical boundaries. This is the "default state" for all human beings, regardless of their social status, financial position, level of intelligence, academic or scientific prestige, honors, physical prowess, or life experience.

In this default state, it can be quite easy when going about mundane, everyday tasks such as eating, walking, or buying groceries, to be lulled into the belief that we know perfectly who we are or what it is like to be "I."

But do we really know who we are?

"Who am I?" is the old dictum that humanity has been asking since time immemorial. It is the most important question we can ask ourselves.

Many have tried to answer this question through intellectual effort, logic, analysis, and so on, but the chief means of Self-knowledge that still prevails today is spiritual practice/meditation. Pragmatically employing the art of spirituality through practice is the way.

Spiritual practice is the whole-being endeavor of finding out who we truly are. Since people's minds are always full of thoughts and noise resulting from their chaotic lifestyles, they never allow themselves a calm and relaxing moment to look within and deeply self-investigate what or who they are.

Therefore, most seekers have to start the meditative process by putting in tremendous, consistent effort to dig through their mental mess, constantly losing their attention and awareness, and gently coming back over and over again to their practice and point of focus.

Meditation or spiritual practice will, in the long run, lead every seeker to an experience of profound tranquility, spaciousness, and joy. If properly done, it awakens a stillness of being that is so profound that it leaves no question as to whether it is our natural state or not.

The physical body also receives great benefits through meditation: the breathing, blood pressure, metabolism, and heart rate slow down along with the thinking processes (and all of them can even temporarily subside during some yogic techniques).

However, our culture leaves little free time for this self-discovery, so you will have to create this for yourself amidst your probably busy life. If you are reading this book, you are probably already practicing some form of meditation. Make sure it's a proper practice (i.e., one that leads you to profound stillness so that you can abide in the presence of awareness). If you haven't started practicing yet, this is a call to begin. Any practice is better than nothing[17]!

It is not about sitting down and having an experience and then putting that aside and going on with life. It is about uniting and integrating that experience with your whole life; it is about realizing that life is the blissful silent stillness of being that is undifferentiated from the deep state of being that you experience while practicing. That's the natural state of our true Self.

---

[17] You can find a Kriya Yoga routine in *Kriya Yoga Exposed*, or a Kundalini Yoga routine in *Kundalini Exposed*. But you can also do pretty much any other spiritual practice, as long as the source from whence it came is genuine and well-structured. How do you know whether some source is legitimate or not? Well, in the beginning, you don't, mainly because you lack discernment. So just take it from those who your intuition seems to align with, and from those whom upon reading or hearing their teachings, you feel peace and a state of well-being.

WHEN TAPAS IS ALL THERE IS

All spiritual practices require a genuine connection with our internal dimension, otherwise they will be dry, barren, and devoid of grace and joy. They must never become a chore.

Spiritual practice is not a mechanical activity, but one that should be very alive, fresh, and lucid. Whenever you do it just for the sake of doing it, or because you've taken a vow or made a promise, there will be a high chance of that session being a shallow meditation.

Furthermore, people often believe that a serious and consistent practice of meditation should be done (or it will be better if done) in a remote location, alone, and totally detached from interacting in and with the world. For this reason, many seekers who desire to engage in a long or continuous meditative practice, do so (unconsciously) as a form of escapism[18]. Suffering is not to be escaped, but to be defeated.

You mustn't try to shut down life and use meditation as a form of escape. You will not go far if you do so. Meditation is a process (to achieve the realization of who we truly are),

---

[18] Escapism can be seen as a propensity to seek distraction and relief from our issues or from the unpleasant parts of our life. Most of "entertainment" can be seen as a form of escapism.

rather than a goal in itself (escaping from life's issues and problems).

It's not about attempting to overlook our human existence and its problems, but instead it's about overcoming those problems and embracing and bathing our human existence with the peace that is inherent to our very core.

Meditation must be a reflection of life itself. As we purify our mind and manage to bring our meditative state into daily life, the whole of life itself will become a meditation or spiritual practice.

There will be many disturbances from outside (people, work, events, society, media, etc.), in addition to the distractions that occur from within (thoughts, emotions, etc.)—but you have to plunge through. See these as positive hurdles that will show you how stable the spiritual depth is that you've integrated into your life, or how profound your mindfulness has become.

"The life you lead conceals the light you are."
- Sri Aurobindo

The majority of our daily life is primarily done on auto-pilot through some form of routine. Routines have their purpose and they can be quite useful. If you go to sleep and wake up at the same time every day, you won't need an alarm clock. You've taught your body and mind the correct times to fall asleep and wake up. This is really useful because you'll always wake up refreshed and ready to tackle the day. There's no problem with this whatsoever. You can constructively apply different conditionings to different things, such as always doing sitting practice at the same time, which conditions your mind to enter into a meditation-prone state quickly.

The problem arises in other forms of auto-pilot or routines. If you take the same route to work every day, for example, regardless of whether this is done by car, bike, foot, or public transportation, there's a high probability that your body will do what is required to travel the path, but your mind—because it doesn't have to exert nearly any conscious effort to travel the path—will be free to wander. And what happens then? You get lost in thoughts or daydreaming, and are not using the free time in a conscious and attentive way.

If the mind is not consistently brought back to the present moment, it will habitually drift toward the past or future. This phenomenon is not new—you've probably been aware of it before. If you witness this attentively, you will notice how rarely you are present throughout the day. Even if you do stop the mind and try to be present for a while, you may find the mind sliding into judgments, narrations, or labeling what it is currently perceiving.

Living mindfully is being present at every moment rather than being absent and letting your life be lived by your mechanical habits and reactions. Sitting practice is what will give you the ability to commit every moment to being fully present throughout the rest of the day. It's a catalyst that enables you to experience a state of pure equanimity which grows and expands from the depths of your inner peace, embracing your life and of those who come in contact with you. *Tapas is your life. You don't do it—you become one with it.*

CHAPTER 9

SVADHYAYA
THE UNIVERSITY OF BEING

Svadhyaya is the study of one's self. *Sva* means "one's own," or "self," and a*dhyaya* means "lesson," or "entering into." Together, they literally form the word "self-study," though it is often interpreted to mean the "study of sacred scriptures" because such scriptures teach about the self and how to transcend it.

Sometimes, it is also understood as a "recitation of mantras." However, our focus here is on the study of our self. It's not about reading scriptures or chanting mantras, but about launching a probe into our inner world—into "I."

But who is "I"?

Who or what is the self?

We Are Not The Children of Dead Matter

The value of your stock portfolio has been on the rise for many years or decades by now. It's gotten steady returns each year, and thus you keep re-investing the dividends. However, sooner or later, once you decide to withdraw or cash out, you will be in for a surprise.

What is this portfolio I'm talking about? Which companies' stocks are in it?

Well, first of all, we have to understand that your investment portfolio manager goes by the name of "ego." His main investments are on the idea of being a separate self-governing entity, and on beliefs, assumptions, creeds, and spiritual doctrines obtained from gurus and books.

Do you really want to stay with this investment strategy? Are you sure that your retirement plan is in good hands? How should you proceed from now on?

Let's start with the primary investment, which is the core belief: "I am the body."

Is this true? When you hurt some part of your body, you say, "My [insert body part here] hurts." I.e., "My head hurts," "My knee aches," "My teeth are killing me." Sometimes, you can also say, "I [the body] am in pain."

Are you your body? Does "I" = body?

You can say "I" when talking about the body, such as "I am tall," but you can also talk about the body as "it," such as "My body's temperature is really high."

What do we, as human beings, even mean when we say "I am the body"? If we have hair and then shave it off, did something happen to us? Do we still feel "I am the body"? Yes?

Ok, then we are not the "hair" right?

What about our limbs? What if someone has to have their arm amputated? Did something happen to that person? Yes, they lost an arm, but does that person still feel "I am the body"? Yes?

Ok, so then we are not the arm either, or any other limbs for that matter.

Are we the heart? If our heart stops beating, the body dies, right? So, whenever we feel "I am the body," are we talking about the heart? What about the lungs? Ok, so there are some critical parts without which our body just cannot continue living.

Do we think that we are the heart, the brain, or the lungs whenever we feel "I am the body"? Nobody would say so.

So what are we really conveying with the belief "I am the body"? Perhaps it feels like we are "something" that lives "inside" the physical body?

What is the "physical body" anyway? With the exception of our head, we can see the whole body with our eyes, which are themselves part of it. We can only see our head through a reflection. Perhaps we can see our nose, eyebrows, lips, or cheekbones, but no one ever saw their forehead or eyes without looking at a reflection.

We can also use our hands, feet, arms, and legs, which themselves are part of the physical body as well, to touch it. We use the tactile sense for that, which provides us with physical sensations of the skin, teeth, hair, and so on. Additionally, we also utilize the proprioceptive sense to know where our limbs are in space.

So, what we know about the physical body through our direct experience, so far, is that it is something that we partially see (that we can touch with some parts of the body itself) that seems to be separated from everything else, which we can call "what-is-not our body." There are also lots of things that the physical body can do, such as inhaling or exhaling air, ingesting or excreting matter, etc. Ok, what else?

Science says that our bodies are composed of about 55-65%

water. Do we feel like a "water body"? I guess not. We're trying to decipher what the feeling "I am the body" means, rather than scientifically understanding what the body is composed of or its mechanisms.

What else is the feeling "I am the body" composed of?

Inner sensations? Yes. Whatever we feel inside (feelings, emotions, etc.), these are only sensations that we perceive. Some sensations can be quite powerful, like the sensation of being localized inside the body, and even more prevalent, the sensation that our awareness is emanating from the inside of our head, as if the head were the headquarters of our experience of being a body.

Are thoughts considered part of the "I am the body" experience? If so, where are they? In the head? If someone were to open your skull, would they find your thoughts in there? Ok, so this is just another layer of sensation, the sensation of thoughts being localized inside our head.

On the other hand, if thoughts are not considered part of the "I am the body" experience because they are not the "body" itself, then we are not our thoughts, right? They just pop up and disappear, although sometimes they seem to drop an anchor in the sea of our mind and linger a little longer.

What we said for thoughts can apply to feelings and emotions in a similar fashion. Sometimes they may be felt in our head, sometimes in our solar plexus, sometimes in the heart area, etc. Would anyone find emotions or feelings there? No, they are just perceived sensations.

So what really is our body? Perceptions and sensations?

What is this "something" that seems to live inside the physical body? It's something that is aware of perceptions, sensations, and thoughts. This "something" that is aware of all of that is not these things, but rather, it is that which is aware of them.

If we are more than just a bundle of cells structured into blood, flesh, and bones; if we are more than just a collection of beliefs, thoughts, feelings, and emotions; if we are more than just perceptions and sensations, then we have to find out what we are.

What is this "something"? Does it live inside the body? Does it die like the body, or is it even born? Where does this "something" come from? Is it a byproduct of the brain, like materialistic science seems to suggest?

Is this "something"—which we can call consciousness or awareness—in the brain, which in turn is in the head, in the body, and in the world?

Believing that consciousness is a by-product of the brain

is a perplexing act of logic that refutes the existence of consciousness itself. The predominant worldview assumes that the Big Bang brought about matter, which eventually evolved into the world, the body, and the brain, out of which consciousness then emerged. But can you ever confirm this? You first need consciousness to confirm or verify anything at all—which makes consciousness the primary substrate of all things.

Can you understand this critical point? Take away consciousness—and you take away everything. Are there any thoughts or ideas about the Big Bang or anything at all when there seems to be no consciousness, like when you are in deep dreamless sleep or passed out? No, there aren't. It is only when you wake up (when you seem to regain consciousness) that such thoughts, ideas, or observations can arise. This means that they are all preceded by consciousness.

The idea or concept of the Big Bang arises *in* consciousness. The existence of anything requires consciousness of that very thing to validate its relative existence. Could we ever know about the existence of anything without consciousness? All experience or knowing comes from consciousness. Nothing can ever be known or experienced without consciousness; thus everything that is known arises *in* consciousness.

This is what you have to find out for yourself. Unraveling

this mystery of our "Self" will unveil the mystery of consciousness and God. That's why you've enrolled in this spiritual journey—to find out that you are not and have never been a child of dead matter.

Finding Out the "Me" That You Are

Most human beings have spent their entire lives scarcely surviving. They seem to be fine, living life with a mask that changes depending on the circumstances and with whom they are interacting. But is it all a façade?

Typically, there is a turmoil inside people. They do their best to hide it from others and especially from themselves. Deep down, despite the subtle lies, regardless of how perfectly they try to hide it from themselves or others, they just know it.

But has anyone ever stopped to wonder what it is like to be themselves?

What is it like to be you? What does it feel like living within that body?

Try to be aware of what it is like to be you. This is not an easy answer. It is perfectly okay if you don't know the answer. You may take a few minutes, hours, or even days to do this. There's no hurry. What I want from this inquiry is for you to understand that the life you've been living so far is probably not up to your highest potential.

Despite what one might think, 99.99% of humanity is not winning in the game of life. No, not even those who have achieved tremendous success and prestige, material wealth, or even acquired a massive amount of knowledge. Such a game of life always ends up in death. We, on the other hand, are not interested in "winning" at life or avoiding death. Rather, we are interested in realizing what is beyond both—what is unborn, and thus deathless.

What is it like to be you?

* * *

Did it seem impossible to know what is it like to be you?

Did that inquiry bring up a spaciousness, a feeling of emptiness, a sense of tranquility, a void of nothingness, or a warm and joyful tactile sensation centered around the heart? There are various possible experiences that may occur when attempting to answer this question, but with any of them, we should remain with these experiences and investigate deeper into the experiencer itself.

Or conversely, this inquiry may have brought up painful bodily sensations, uncomfortable feelings, or uneasy experiences, typically associated with the practitioner's personal story or deep-rooted psychological issues. Moreover, most people, when asked such a question, will automatically answer with different characteristics, traits, or personality-related attributes, as if those were what constitutes who they are. But we know that's not correct.

If you could not grasp the "What is it like to be you?" question from the previous chapter, then you simply need a higher degree of awareness. You can achieve that through spiritual practice.

You will experience different layers of "You"; it all depends on what you consider yourself to be. Your experience of "What is it like to be you?" will vary according to one of these following "You's":

(1)
The "You" you think you are (body and personality).

You believe that you are the body-mind, and you identify with everything that appears in your consciousness, from thoughts to emotions.

How to graduate from this level of "You"?

If you are able to observe qualities such as likes, dislikes, habits, patterns of behavior, personality traits, etc., then you can't be any of those. You may say, "I am sad" whenever thoughts and emotions of sadness arise in you. But are you really sad, or are you just identifying with the thoughts, emotions, and sensations that you label as "sadness"? Are those thoughts and emotions appearing in the space of consciousness? Don't you perceive them? You observe them emerge and vanish, don't you? That means you stand apart from them. You perceive those thoughts and emotions of sadness. Mindfulness and witnessing allow you to truly realize this, but you need a strong foundation of spiritual practice to really use these tools with sharp efficacy.

(2)
The "You" that controls all of your decisions, actions, speech, and all types of unconscious behaviors and patterns (the identity below the conscious mind).

You believe you are your core identity, which ranges from the conscious mind to more unconscious aspects. You believe you are in control.

How to graduate from this level of "You"?

After consciously realizing the previous state (i.e., you are not that which you can perceive), you need to infuse that insight into all of your being, permeating it into the parts of your subconscious mind where habits, subtle desires, traumas, etc., reside. You have to infuse the light of discernment into the core of your identity, so that you truly realize that you are neither your identity nor your personal story. It's not enough to know that you are not what you perceive (what appears and disappears before your "I"), but also that you are not what seems to constitute your "I," the perceiver, either. All of its deep-rooted facets must be purified.

Advanced spiritual practice enables one to do this the best. Find whatever is untrue in your experience and let go of it. Once it is seen to be false, you cannot continue believing that it is you, and hence it becomes easy and natural to simply drop it. You are not trying to force or get to know that special "True Self" or anything like that; you just want to let go of what you realize is untrue by shedding the illusory false-ness right out of yourself! You are peeling off the "ego-onion."

(3)
The "I-ego," the root false you.

Here you reach the final knot, which is typically called *Chit-Jada-Granthi*[19]. This is the knot that binds consciousness

---

[19] *Chit:* consciousness; *Jada:* that which is insentient or inert; *Granthi:* knot.

to the body. This knot represents the root belief of being an individual entity, and it is severed once you realize your true light of pure awareness. In other words, once you dissolve the wrong identification with the body-mind as being "I," this knot is destroyed.

Basically, after realizing through direct experience (and infusing it as deeply as possible into the kernel of your identity through the subconscious) that you are neither a particular object, nor another, and so on, until there are no objects left for your consciousness to identify with, then you (as consciousness) remain objectless and pure (without "I"). After removing everything, what remains is *What Is*. Staying as *That* is the way. This work is best done within the realm of Self-Inquiry, Self-Awareness, Parvastha, or similar "nondual practices." That's how you graduate into the final level.

> "Truth, like gold, is to be obtained not by its growth, but by washing away from it all that is not gold."
>
> - Leo Tolstoy

(4)
Pure Consciousness—that which is aware—the real You.

The Truth. You are the unbounded and deathless consciousness. That's "You," but obviously not "You" as a person/identity/personality/mind/ego. Rather, it's "You" as an impersonal infinite consciousness, transcending all known and unknown dichotomies of life.

By going through each layer of "You" conditioning, you begin to gain insights into your life, personality, behavior, thinking patterns, mind, and eventually, consciousness itself. At the bottom of the rabbit hole you will discover and realize your true Self. This is the real and pragmatic use of Svadhyaya, the study of being!

CHAPTER 10

ISHVARA PRANIDHANA
THE RELINQUISHMENT

This is the last Niyama, and for me, the most important one. *Ishvara* can take on a varied spectrum of meanings, depending on the context (it differs based on the era and the philosophy of each school of Yoga/Hinduism), such as "personal God," "God with form," "King," "Supreme Guru," "Supreme Being," "Ruler of the Universe," or just "God." Ishvara is translated as "The Best of Rulers" or "The Owner of Choices," but there are way too many contradictions and disputes over the semantics of this word. In this last Niyama, rather than seeing Ishvara as separate from us (i.e., "God with form") we shall see it as "God in us," or "God as us"—the infinite consciousness.

Pranidhana, on the other hand, simply means to "surrender," "devote," "dedicate," or "submit." Ishvara pranidhana thus means to "surrender to God," "devote to the Supreme Guru," or "dedicate to the Supreme Being." Literally, the words composing this Niyama signify "submit to the Owner of Choices." This means "surrender your life to The Best of Rulers."

When you surrender the false self to God—the true Self[20]; when you surrender your personal self to the impersonal Transcendence—you give all your choices away. In other words, anything that happens, it's okay. You will neither reject nor embrace it because it's all God's will. This is surrendering your entire life to God. It's the path of surrender—letting yourself go as a wave in the ocean, knowing that the ocean takes care of you. After all, you yourself are the ocean; you just aren't fully aware of it yet. This is the stuff that the lives of saints are made of.

According to Maharishi Patanjali, out of all the Yamas and Niyamas, this last Niyama is the most essential one because of its tremendous power to catapult you to Samadhi—the final goal of Yoga. It is *that* important.

"From surrender to God, comes the ultimate Samadhi."

- MAHARISHI PATANJALI,
THE YOGA SUTRAS

---

[20] There aren't two selves. This is a way of expounding the Truth, relatively speaking.

GOD IS NOT A CELEBRITY

Surrendering ourselves to God is vital to the process of the perfection of Yoga. All of the Yamas and Niyamas (and the rest of limbs that comprise Maharishi Patanjali's system[21]) must be directed and surrendered toward God.

Most people in the world worship celebrities. *Celebrity* comes from the Latin *celibritatem*, which is related to "celebration," "populous." When fans meet their idol, they have hysterical reactions. They put their idol up on a pedestal, and when they meet him/her, they go into a trance-like state of submission and a "melting-worship-devotion." If those fans were able to spend an entire day with their idol, they'd be in a state of surrender-devotion, their eyes filled with joy and fascination. This is similar to what used to happen in the ancient days when simple peons met royalty.

I once happened to see a famous "TV star" visit the ashram of a very known eastern guru, and he was mesmerized by how people treated that guru as a god. "You are a god to these people!" or "You are like royalty!" were some of the utterances that the TV star said in disbelief. He couldn't

---

[21] The eight limbs of Yoga are: Yama, Niyama, Asana, Pranayama, Pratyahara, Dharana, Dhyana, and Samadhi.

believe how so many people could devote, surrender, and worship a guru like that.

What the TV star didn't recognize, however, is that this was exactly how people back in western society treated him and other "celebrities." They are treated like gods or royalty.

People treat celebrities like that because they envision famous people as having what they think they want: wealth, success, social status, power, etc. They want some of that as well.

Why was this TV star so shocked to see other people treating their guru as a god? These disciples treat their guru like that because they envision their guru as having what they think they want: spiritual wealth, happiness, peace, wisdom, etc.

These disciples are not looking for material wealth, but rather spiritual wealth; and they measure success as having realized their inherent unity with God, with the pure boundless happiness that they are. They were actually doing the exact same behaviors as people in western societies; it's just that the type of wealth and success that they are looking for is different, and thus the meaning of "celebrity" there is also different. Lack of discernment can be a pretty big blind spot, one that this TV star obviously possessed.

I also see people treating God as the ultimate celebrity. But God doesn't want to be treated like a celebrity. God doesn't need your rituals or offerings. God doesn't want to be placed up on a pedestal; God doesn't need or lack anything. But God should be celebrated nonetheless—with your total devotion, worship, and surrender.

These three are not different—they all mean that you, as an apparent individual awareness, should devote, worship, and surrender to your own awareness. After all, before any idea or thought of God arises, "I" has to be there—consciousness has to be there. Finding out what this consciousness is will ultimately lead you to the realization of the infinite consciousness that God is—and that you are. This is the ultimate surrender of self (individual consciousness) to God (infinite consciousness).

THE SCIENCE OR ART OF SELF-REALIZATION?

There are many forms of meditation, and I have found that two of the most powerful ones are Kriya Yoga and Kundalini Yoga. They provide a fertile ground for our minds so that we can realize our immortal origin and timeless essence, wherein our individual consciousness "goes back" to whence it came, "reuniting" with God.

Many people call spiritual practice a "science"—the science of Self-Realization. I have a few issues with such a description. First of all, there is no perfect formula that guarantees that an individual consciousness will "return" to its source and realize its true nature, if it follows that formula to the letter. Just look at the fact that most disciples of gurus or organizations who purport this to be true haven't become Self-Realized. Why is that? Because some things just can't be quantified.

Let's take a look at chess. Chess is a game where all of the information is present at all times—there are no unknown variables or hidden information. It's all known. There may come a time when a super ultra-advanced quantum computer will be able to solve chess in its entirety. Theoretically, it is possible to develop a formula to never lose at chess (though impossible at the moment because of computational limitations), or checkers (the latter of which has already been done[22]).

However, we cannot do that with Self-Realization[23]. This is because some factors cannot be measured or quantified. Among them, the essential one that simply cannot be measured is surrender.

I've mentioned surrender in all of my books. This is because surrender is the secret essential ingredient that makes all this journey and practice actually work. The intense desire for Freedom that I've mentioned in a previous chapter is intimately connected with surrender—they go hand-in-hand. As your desire to know yourself increases, so does your surrender. They are basically the same—the greater the desire, the greater the surrender, just like the more gasoline you pour into a fire, the longer and stronger it will burn.

---

[22] https://science.sciencemag.org/content/317/5844/1518

[23] But we can certainly call it a "science" if we are talking about attaining the experience of bliss, peace, ecstasy, wisdom, lucid dreaming, out-of-body projections, visions, etc. Precise instructions can be given that can lead a seeker to different states of consciousness, where such experiences can be had, yet none of them are Self-Realization. It's important to understand the difference.

Surrender has to be infinite—that's how one can become enlightened! If your surrender is still not infinite, you will not realize your true essence.

In our lives, we typically carry around the baggage, hardships, and traumas of our personal stories, as well as our current sources of anxiety and problems. When we perform spiritual practice, we must let go of all these unnecessary burdens. If we can let them go without looking back, we feel freer, more alive, and younger, and our meditation will then go much deeper.

However, regardless of how profoundly you abandon your personal burdens during meditation, you must go one step further and let go of the one who lets go (the "I"). Sooner or later, this will become the most imperative "step" in your spiritual journey—as it was in mine. It just requires discrimination/discernment.

The relinquishing of the ego is the most transcendental undertaking in the whole of meditation. It is much more difficult than the letting go of your personal burdens, or than paying attention to the breath or restraining the life-force. You can allow yourself to fine-tune your identity (by purifying the mind, letting go of your burdens, acquiring a higher level of concentration, etc.), but letting go of it altogether— that's a different story.

Surrender is a complex process, yet paradoxically simple, which is why the mind has a hard time "getting it." If you are still in the first steps on your spiritual path, you should not put too much emphasis into understanding it; rather, you should do your best to practice according to the instructions. With time, as your power of consciousness increases (i.e., you "attain" a higher level of discernment or insight), you will become more conscious of what surrender is and how to "apply" it[24].

Surrender is one of the essential aspects of both the yogic and a more general spiritual path. Genuine surrendering doesn't demand rituals, worshiping figures, or anything of a similar nature—it is much deeper than that. It is the unceasing "act" of letting go "toward" your own Self.

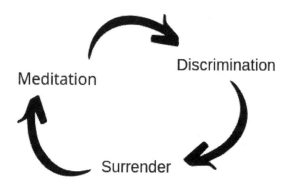

---

[24] Refer to *The Secret Power of Kriya Yoga*, chapter 8 "The Art of Nondual Bhakti" for a bhakti-surrender approach to Kriya Yoga practice, or to *Turiya: The God State*, chapter 8 "Shedding Light Into True Surrender" to a very advanced form of surrender during nondual spiritual practice.

Meditation awakens discrimination, which in turn gives rise to the "ability" to properly surrender, which in turn increases the power of meditation, which increases discrimination, making surrender even more powerful, and so on. This cycle goes on and on until all three merge into one and become the perfect ground for enlightenment.

It can be said that you can put any of the Yamas and Niyamas into one of these three (meditation, discrimination, or surrender). Can you do it? It's a fun exercise that requires some degree of awareness, but it can help you see how everything is interlinked.

When they become one, you will have successfully graduated from all of the Yamas and Niyamas presented in this book. That's the whole purpose—to unify them!

With the perfect ground for enlightenment having been established, it's inevitable that you will realize your true nature. After all, it's your ultimate destiny—one that not even you can deny.

The Truth about Grace

Imagine that you have a rubber ball in your hand. If you squeeze it, it will contract, but as soon as you let go, it will spring back to its original spherical shape.

Surrender is letting go of this contraction, allowing the natural state to unfold.

Your inherent desire for happiness, which is your true state of being, is Grace in action. Grace is precisely like the rubber ball going back to its original state. It's akin to the force always pushing the ball to restore its original form. The squeeze, on the other hand, is your individual consciousness, a contraction of the original state. Every time you immerse yourself in Maya, it's like the squeeze on the rubber ball.

But even though you may think you are an individual consciousness, this individuation is just a reflection of the transpersonal consciousness. The consequence of this individuation, of this contraction, is searching for happiness (searching for the original state, the pristine spherical form of the ball). If you seek happiness in Maya through materiality, relationships, status, or anything related to form and duality, you are paradoxically trying to get the ball to its original state by squeezing it further. This obviously won't work. What works is recognizing that the "pull" to the original state is ever-present, and to then stop resisting it.

Grace is ever-present, but it is often neglected or ignored. However, when you transcend into a higher level of consciousness, you realize its omnipresence. Rather than fighting against it by immersing in Maya, you surrender to it. Once you surrender to Grace, it acts faster on you and in a more powerful way, because you are no longer resisting it in its pure state by chasing illusions (squeezing the ball).

Surrendering to Grace is allowing the rubber ball to come back to its natural state, rather than unknowingly forcing it to stay contracted. Surrendering yourself to Grace, which is always pulling you back to your original state, is Ishvara pranidhana.

CHAPTER 11

THE ETERNAL LION

Everything must begin with you. A choice. A decision. A seeking. A longing. A desire. An inspiration. Anything. If you still haven't made the choice, now is a good time to do so. Actually, you've already made it by reading this book—even if you are unaware of it. This is a call from your heart.

Allow yourself to be embraced by your own consciousness, for it will remind you of your eternity. As a body, mind, and individual consciousness, you will not live forever.

It's always good to remember that one day your body will no longer be here. Death is certain. Use this fact to ponder your choices. Every time you choose to go in the direction of Maya, by making a choice that does not propel you further into your self-discovery, you are killing yourself—softly. Every time you choose to go in the direction of realizing the

Truth, by making a choice that propels you further into your self-discovery—you are rebirthing yourself.

By living as a pure vehicle of the light of Awareness, death can't take anything from you. You're already complete! What can death take from one who knows that they are the unborn deathless consciousness? If your experience is already whole, you will never "go before your time" because your experience lies in the realm of the eternal.

This is a real opportunity. The spiritual path is the best path in life, the most tasty and blissful one, but somehow we still seem to not choose it. No one should settle for a counterfeit version of their Self—the true Self is the real and only one.

The Yamas and Niyamas, seen and practiced in the ways explained in this book, will help you to expand and realize your inherent unity with the world and the whole universe. This unity is ever-present, and though it is not self-evident from the typical egoic perspective, it is the only ever-present reality from an enlightened being's view. It is your original and natural state.

Surrendering your individual and finite existence to God—which is pure and infinite Existence itself—may just be the decision that changes your life. Your heart must roar like a lion that wants to be free from its cage!

Wrong will be right, when your own awareness comes in sight,
At the sound of your heart's roar, sorrows will be no more,
When your true colors shine through, winter meets its death,
And when you shake your mane, you shall have spring once again.

So says the eternal lion in you. May spring come!

This book was a manifestation of love, and I hope that it serves you well in your spiritual journey.

If you've enjoyed reading it and if you feel that it has made a positive difference in the way you see the Yamas and Niyamas, please show your support by leaving a *Review on the Amazon page*. It really makes a difference. It helps to spread genuine spiritual teachings to those who are truly seeking them.

Thank you.

Subscribe and receive the ebook **Uncovering the Real** plus updates and information regarding new books or articles, which will be sent about once or twice a month.

www.RealYoga.info

If you have any doubts or questions regarding this or any of the other books, feel free to contact me at:

Santata@RealYoga.info

Read also, by the same author of *The Yogic Dharma*:

— Kriya Yoga Exposed

The Truth About Current Kriya Yoga Gurus & Organizations.

— The Secret Power of Kriya Yoga

Revealing the Fastest Path to Enlightenment. How Fusing Bhakti & Jnana Yoga into Kriya will Unleash the most Powerful Yoga Ever.

— Kundalini Exposed

Disclosing the Cosmic Mystery of Kundalini. The Ultimate Guide to Kundalini Yoga & Kundalini Awakening.

— The Yoga of Consciousness

25 Direct Practices to Enlightenment. Revealing the Missing Key to Self-Realization. Beyond Kundalini, Kriya Yoga & all Spirituality into Awakening Non-Duality.

— Turiya: The God State

Unravel the ancient mystery of Turiya - The God State. The book that demystifies and uncovers the true state of Enlightened beings.

— Samadhi: The Forgotten Eden

Revealing the Ancient Yogic Art of Samadhi.

Available @ Amazon as Kindle & Paperback.

GLOSSARY

Asana – Body posture; a sitting pose for spiritual practice.

Background of Consciousness / Awareness – Another name for pure Awareness. However, such a name presupposes that there is a foreground or that which is witnessed, implying a duality. That's quite right, but it should be understood that this name is a helpful clue for seekers because it helps them take a step back from the mental contents with which they are usually identified, so that they can repose in awareness itself.

Beingness – The intrinsic nature of Consciousness is "Being." To be is to be conscious. At first, "Beingness" might be felt as a profound experience of stillness, peace, joy, etc., but as one goes further, it will dissolve our individuality, and our blissful Oneness will shine through.

Brahman – The Ultimate Reality, the **Absolute**. Some call it **Parabrahman** or **Nirguna Brahman**, which means Highest Brahman or Brahman without form or qualities. It is the **Unmanifested**, which is Awareness devoid of all contents, pure and formless.

Chakra – Wheel/plexus, a psychic-energy center.

Dharana – Concentration.

Dhyana – It's like Dharana, but the concentration is unbroken and steady. It's usually translated as Meditation. In different forms of Buddhism, dhyana can be called *jhana* (in Pali), *chan* (in China) or *zen* (in Japan), although all of these words can also have different meanings depending on the tradition.

Dynamic/Relative consciousness – The manifested side of Consciousness; the relative consciousness.

Ego – "I," the thought "I" or "I-ego." It is the erroneous belief of being a separate being or entity. For a more in-depth understanding, read *The Yoga of Consciousness*.

Energy Body – The subtle body (*Suksma sarira*) is the body between the causal body (*Anandamaya kosha*) and the physical body (*Sthula sarira* or *Annamaya kosha*). According to Vedantic philosophy, it is composed of three "sheaths": **the "energy sheath" (the energy body, *pranamaya kosha; prana or life-force)*,** the "mind sheath" (*manomaya kosha; the mind)*, and the "intellect sheath" (*Vijnanmaya kosha; the intellect or the ability to discriminate)*.

God – Although I have written God as "Himself," God is neither male nor female. God is not a person or an entity—that would make God limited. God is the all-pervading Consciousness, being formless, timeless and unborn. It is the infinite Awareness that each one of us possesses, and out of which everything is "made."

Kriya Supreme Fire – Method to awake the Kundalini, as explained in Kriya Yoga Exposed and Kundalini Exposed

Kundalini – The primal spiritual energy said to be located at the base of the spine. Cosmic Kundalini is the same energy but rather than being the individual's latent energy, it is the universal latent energy, being infinitely more powerful.

Libido – Sexual desire; sex drive.

Mantra – Sacred syllable or word or set of words.

Maya – The veil of illusion that appears to cover our true infinite nature. This veil allows pure empty consciousness to believe it has divided itself into many different forms, each with different qualities, from beings to thoughts to galaxies. It is the **manifested relative**: the contents of Awareness which have manifested from its infinite potential.

Neo-Advaita – A distortion of *Advaita Vedanta* (non-dual school of Hindu philosophy). Proponents of Neo-Advaita teachings affirm that no practice is necessary and that having an enlightenment-experience is enough to be enlightened. Advaita means "not-two."

Prana – Life-force.

Pranayama – Life-force restraint/control technique.

Pratyahara – Pratyahara is the dis-identification of our attention from various external impressions. This refers to disengaging from the physical senses.

Pure Consciousness – Our pure and true formless Self-aware nature. That which is conscious; Is your body conscious? No. Is your brain conscious? No. We could go on all day, until we realize that nothing is conscious by itself, except consciousness. I use Consciousness and Awareness interchangeably throughout this book.

Sadhana – Spiritual Practice.

Samadhi – A higher state of consciousness. It's usually translated as "absorption." If you'd like to learn about the process of **Dharana, Dhyana,** and **Samadhi** from the Yoga Sutras, refer to *Samadhi: The Forgotten Eden*, chapter "The Yogic Samyama."

Self – With a capital "S" means pure Consciousness or pure Awareness, devoid of any objects; self with a small "s" is synonymous with ego or "I."

Sense of Being/I Am – Presence or awareness of existing/of being/ of the background of Consciousness; of that which is aware; Kriya Yoga's Parvastha.

Subconscious mind – That which is beneath the conscious mind. Sometimes, it is also called the "unconscious."

Printed in Great
Britain
by Amazon